AUSTRALIA IN THE WILD

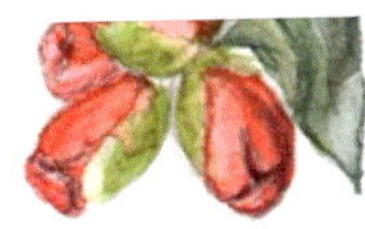

Koala

Kangaroo and joey

Potoroo

Red-necked pademelon

Bilbies (bandicoots)

Platypus

Echidna

Sugar glider

Kookaburra

Galah cockatoo (gang-gang)

Wombat

Tasmanian devil

Numbat

Possum

Wallaby

Spotted quoll

Mallee fowl

Red-tailed black cockatoo

Lyrebird

Cassowary

Emu and chick

Frog-mouthed owl

Wedge-tailed eagle

Australian masked owl

Yellow-crested cockatoos

Rainbow lorikeet

Bowerbirds

Quokka

Frill-necked lizard

Horny devil

Goanna

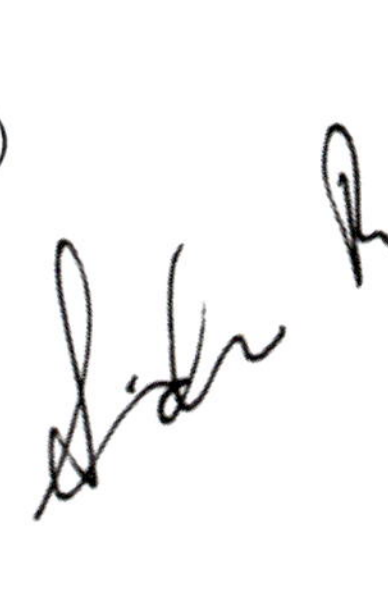

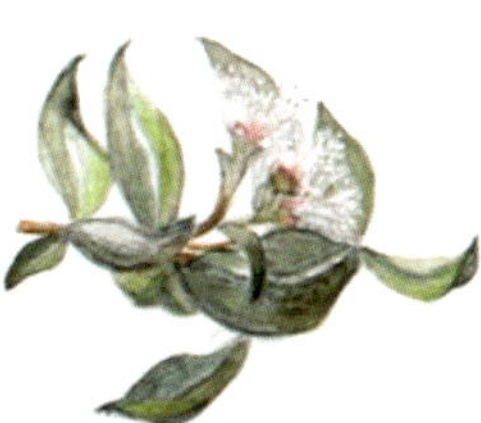

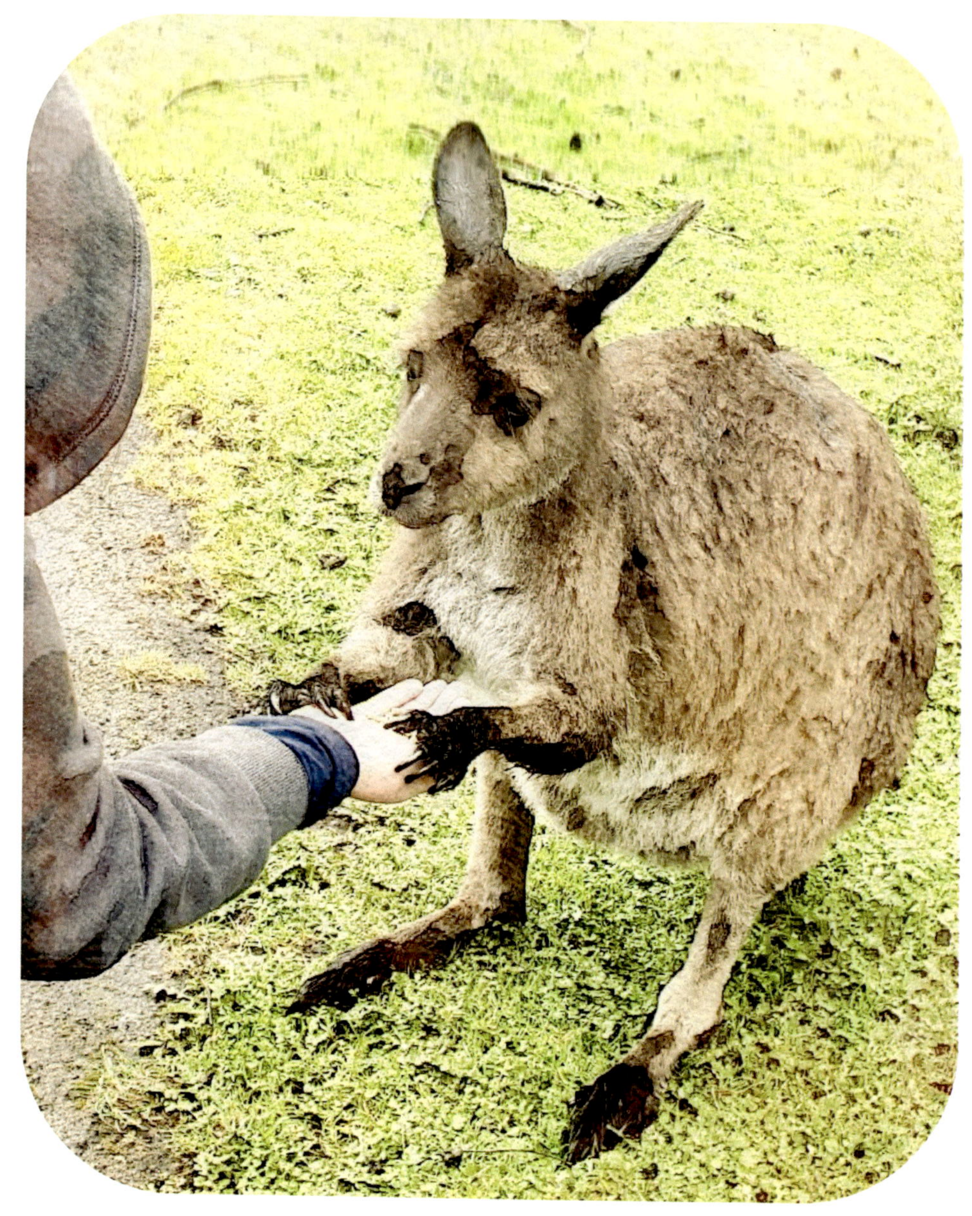

In a land as harsh on its wildlife as its peoples, humans have a unique guardianship for the fauna and flora of the landscape. As a child I hated seeing any creature confined, but during the recent wildfire season we've seen the interdependence between us, as birds and animals have sought our care. Many people responded, with sanctuaries, care stations and animal hospitals springing into action. Australians have prioritised pets and wildlife over property. The world, looking on in horror has reached out—from donations to simple kind acts, like making koala mittens. As Australians, we are island-isolated but with the reaction around the globe, we know we're not alone.

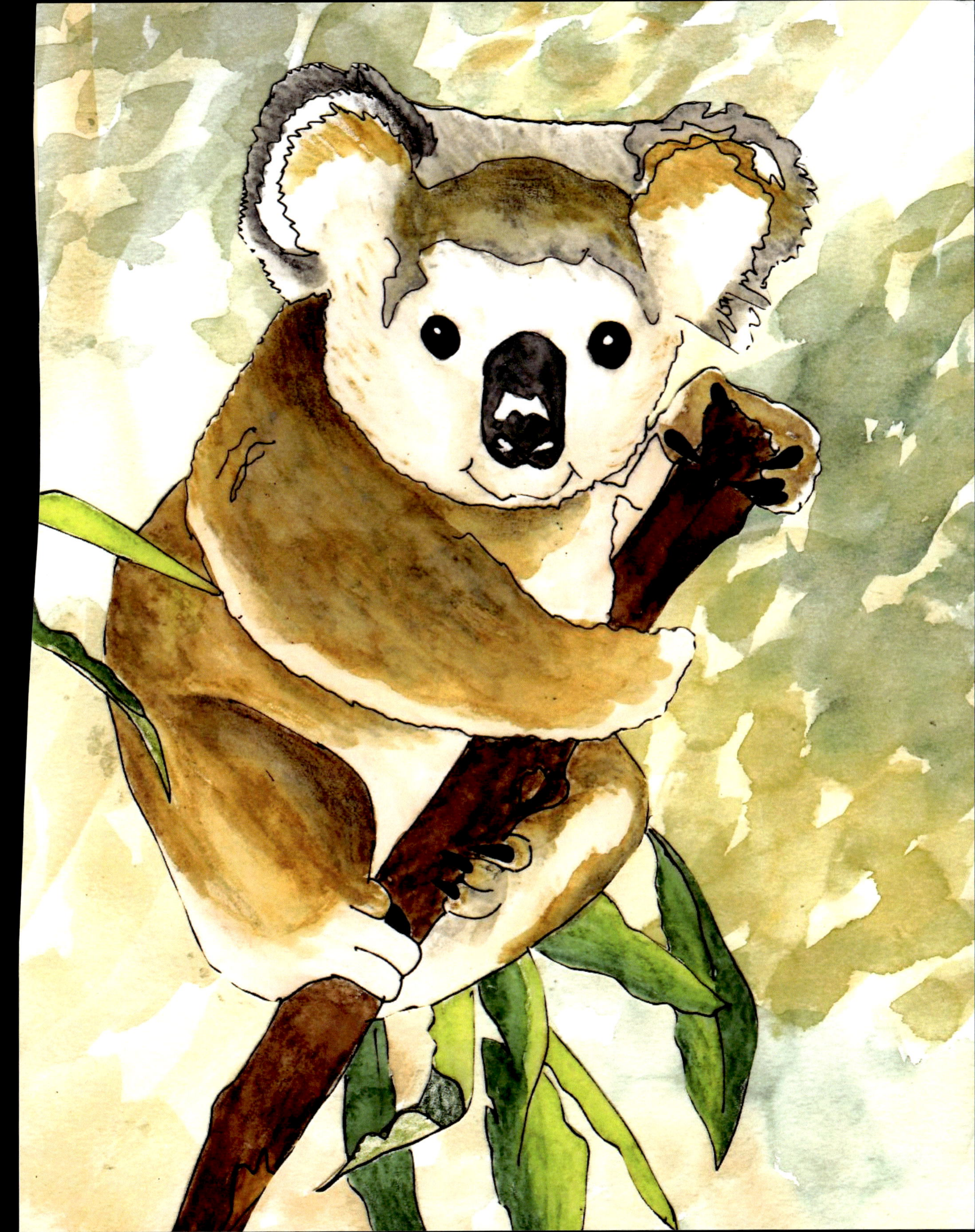

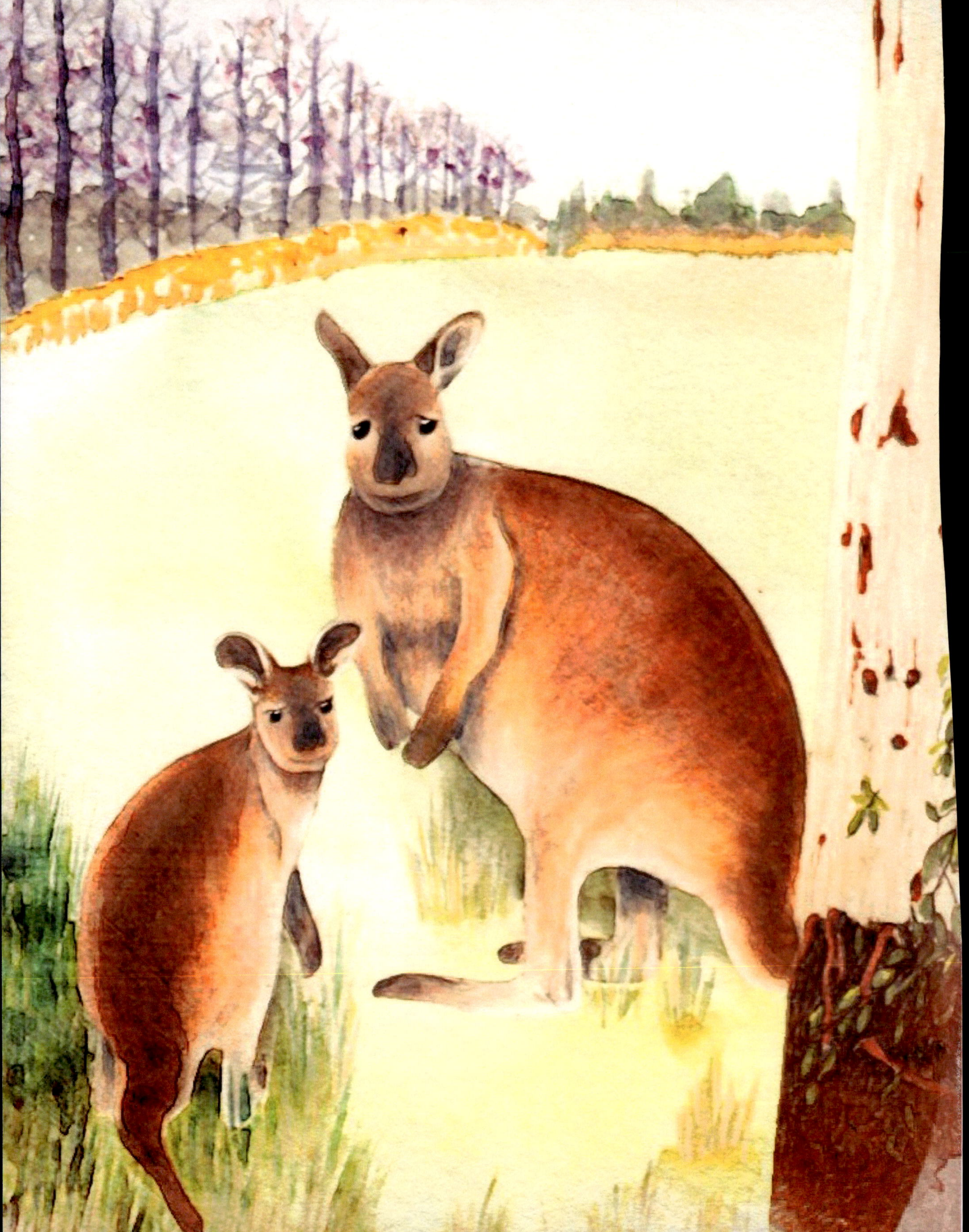

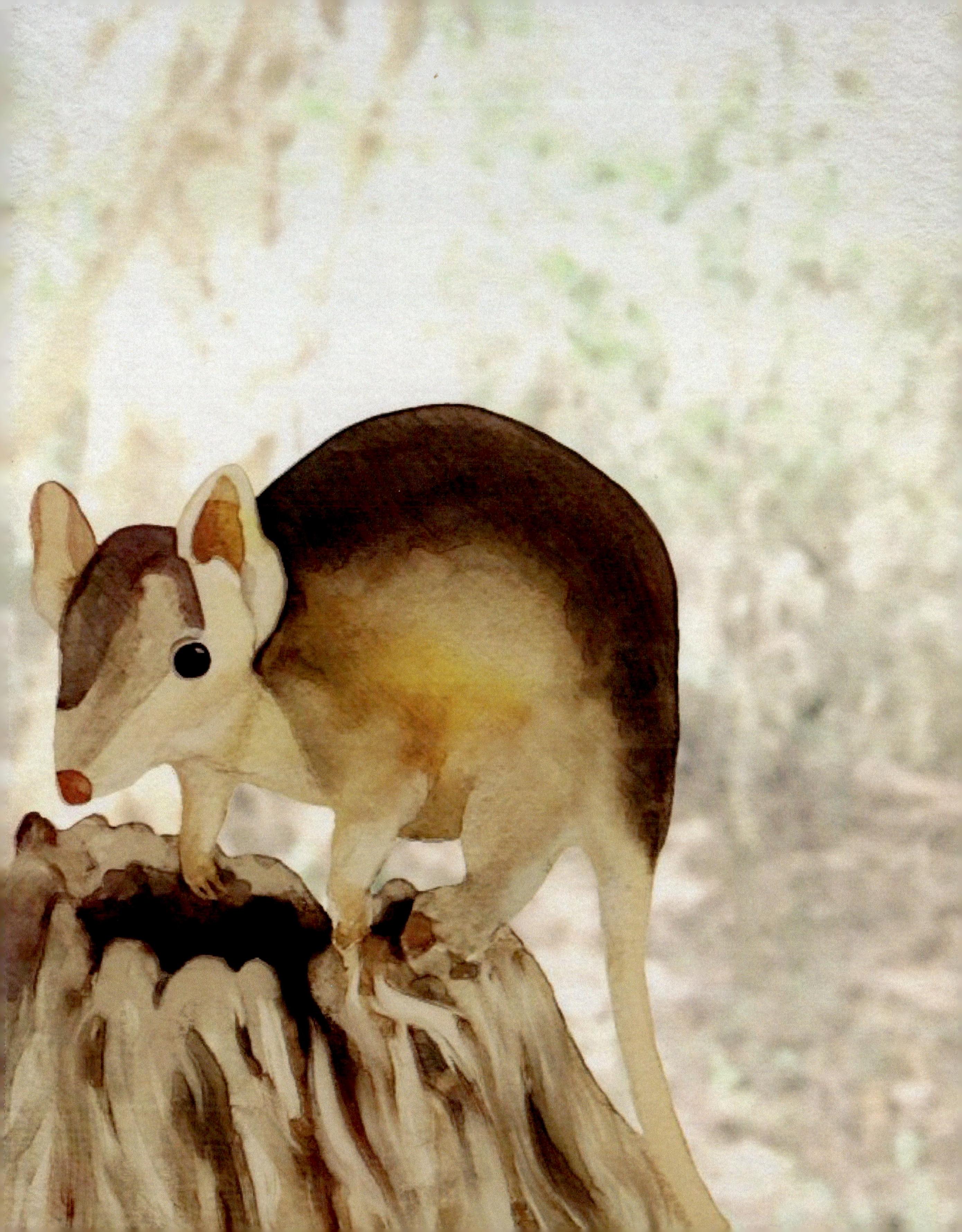

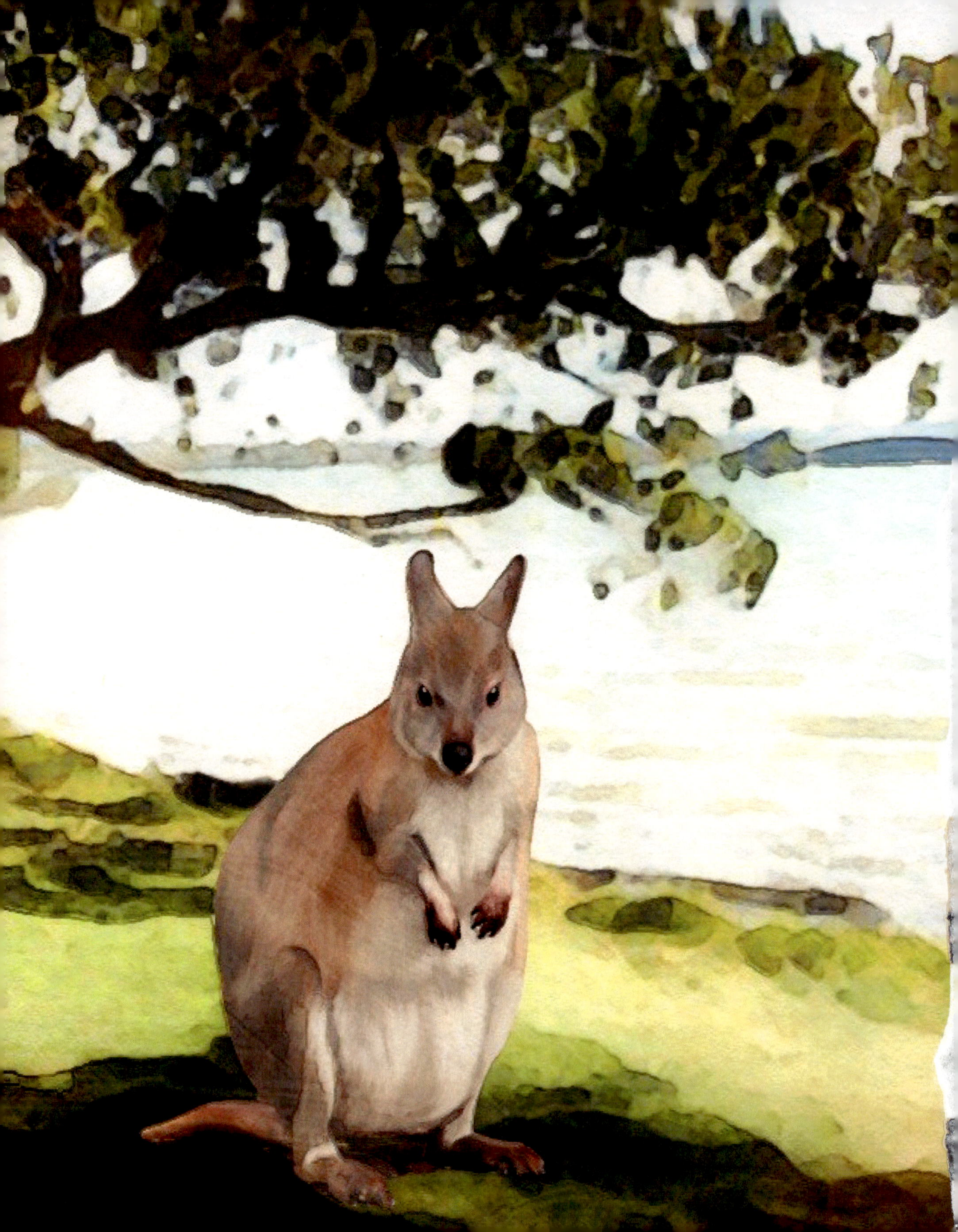

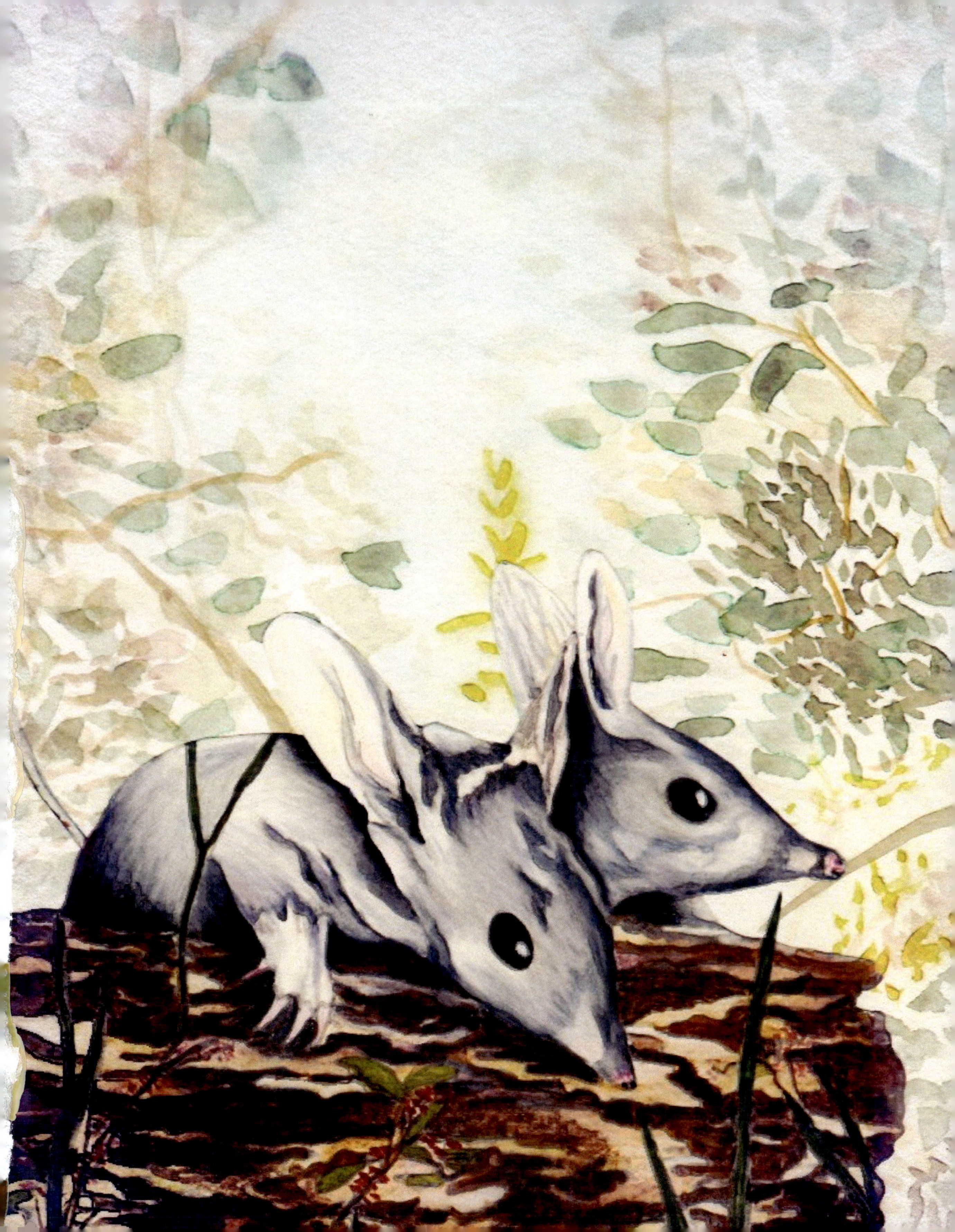

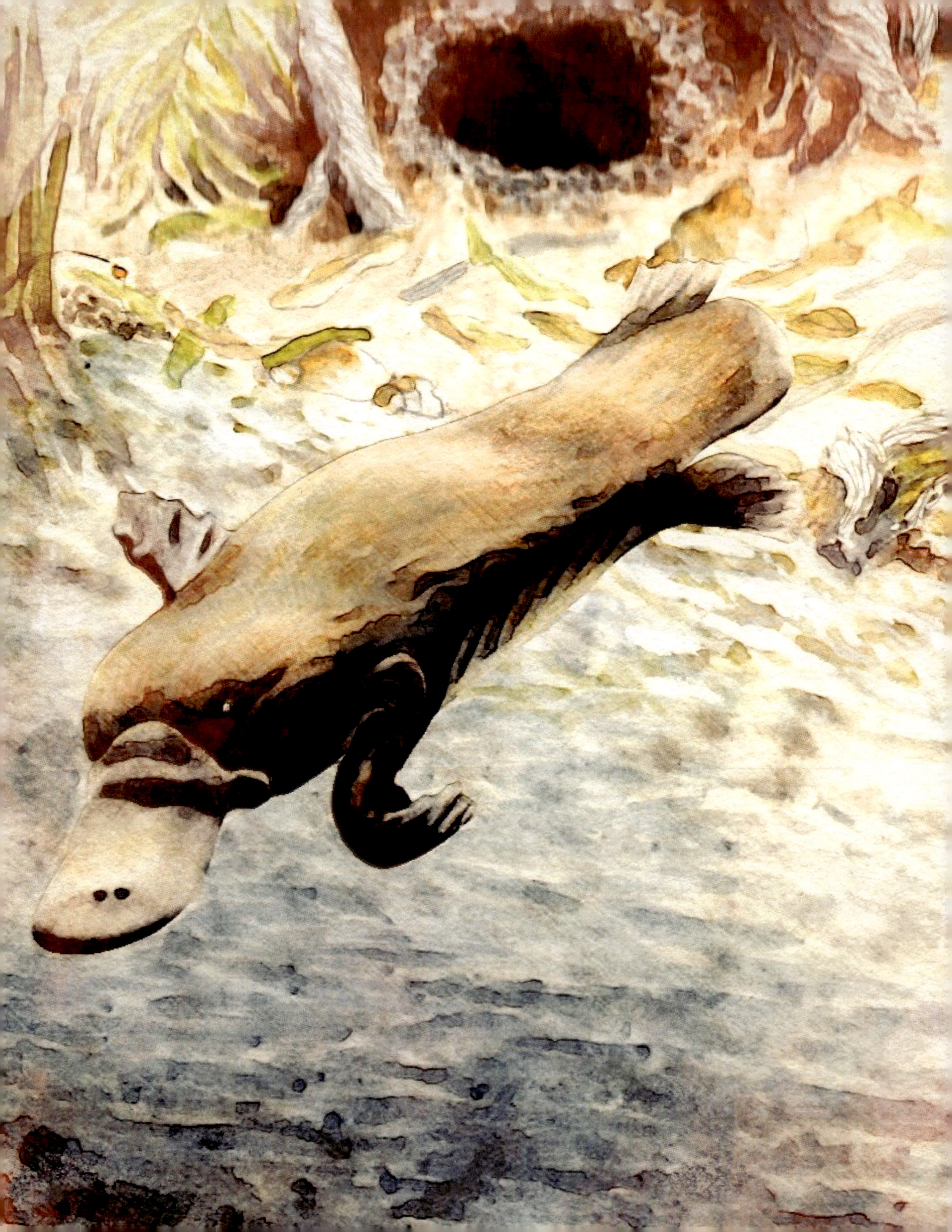

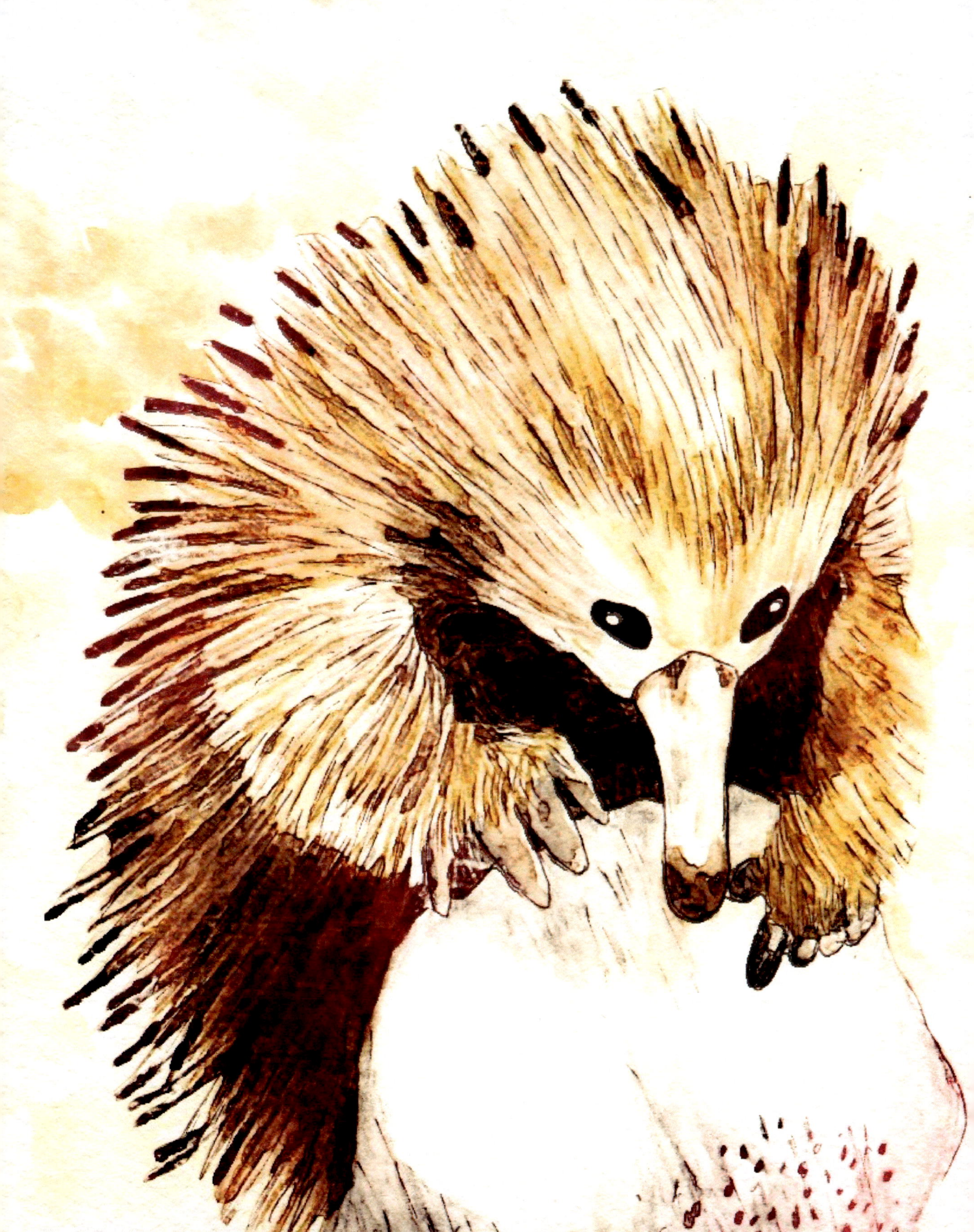

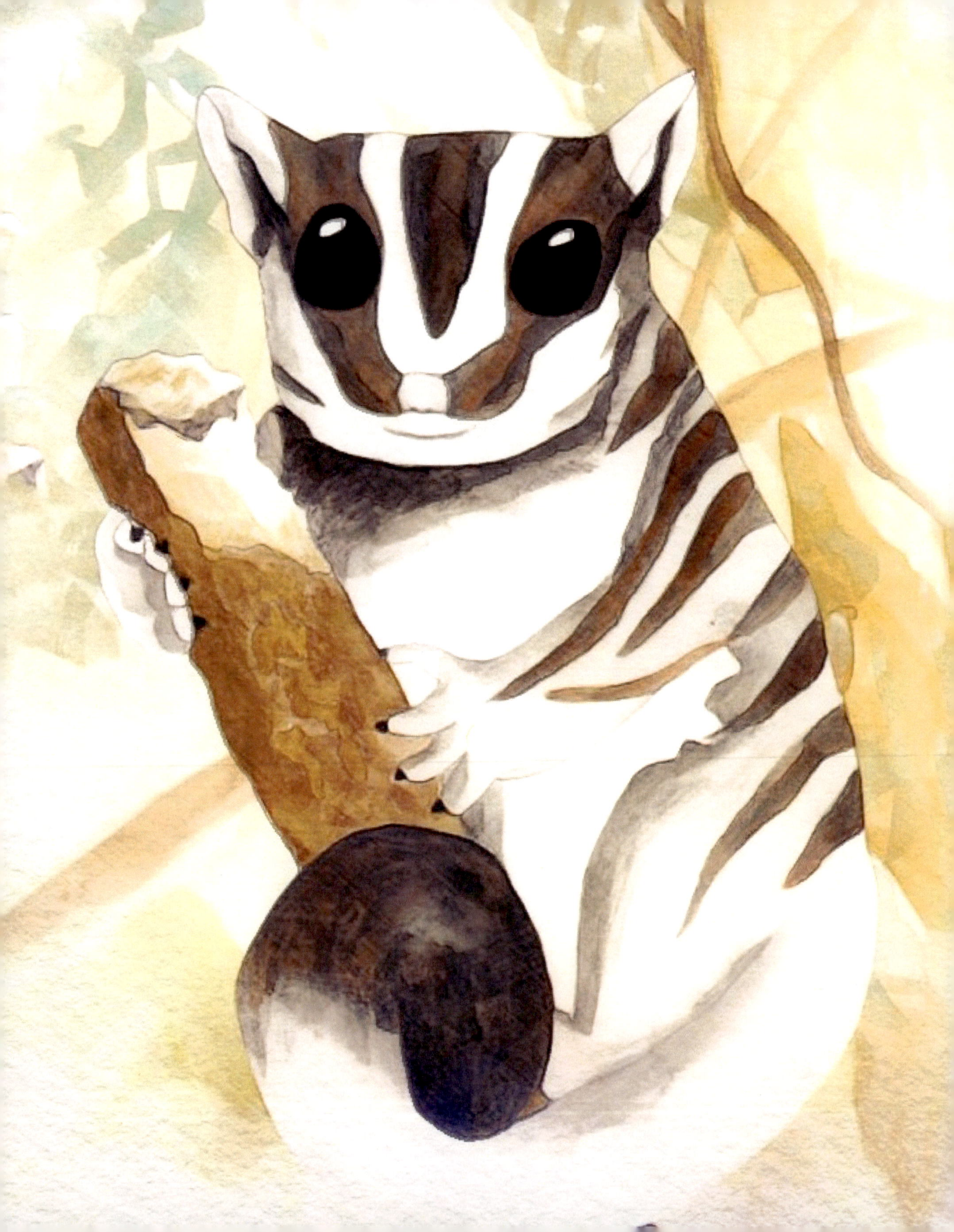

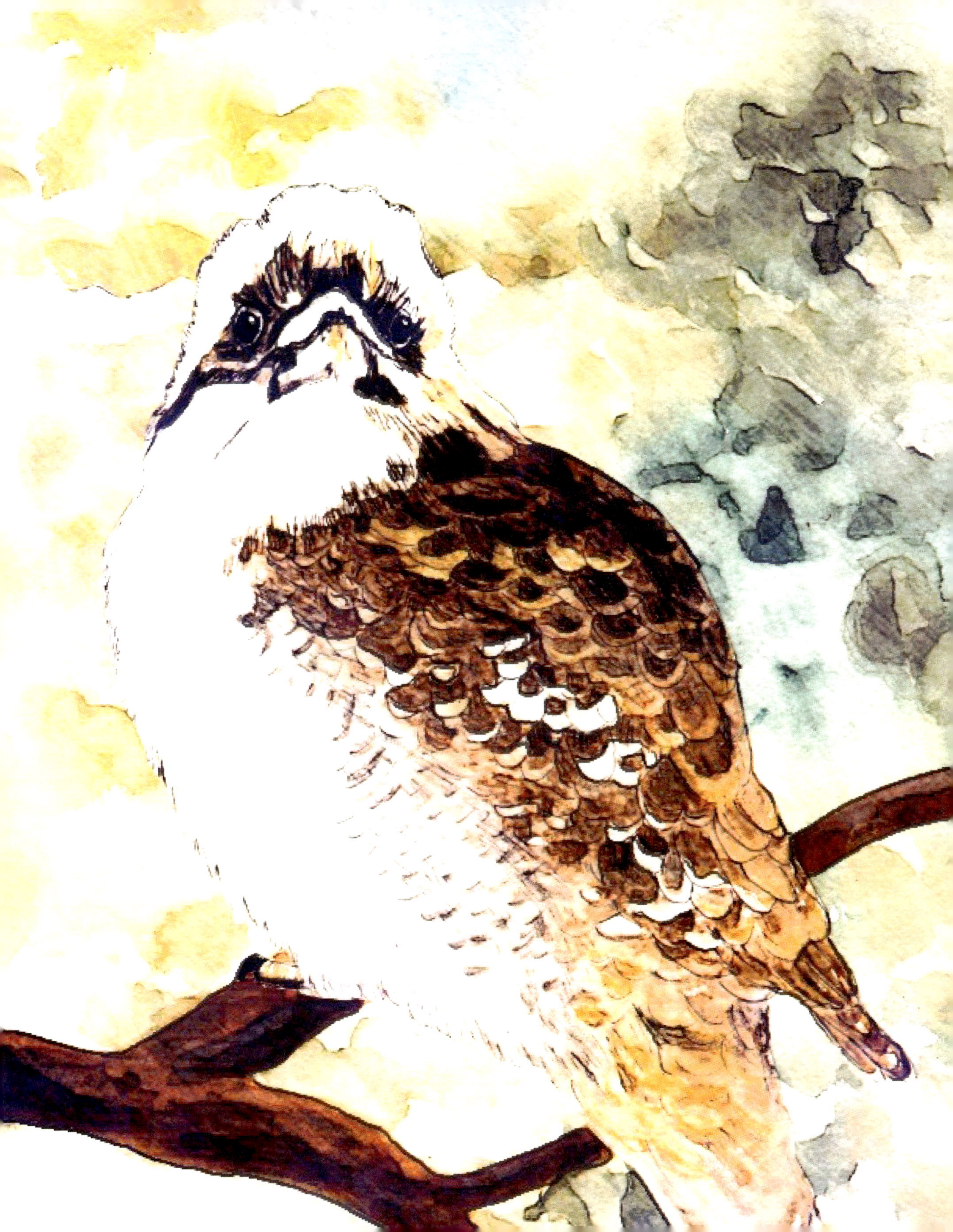

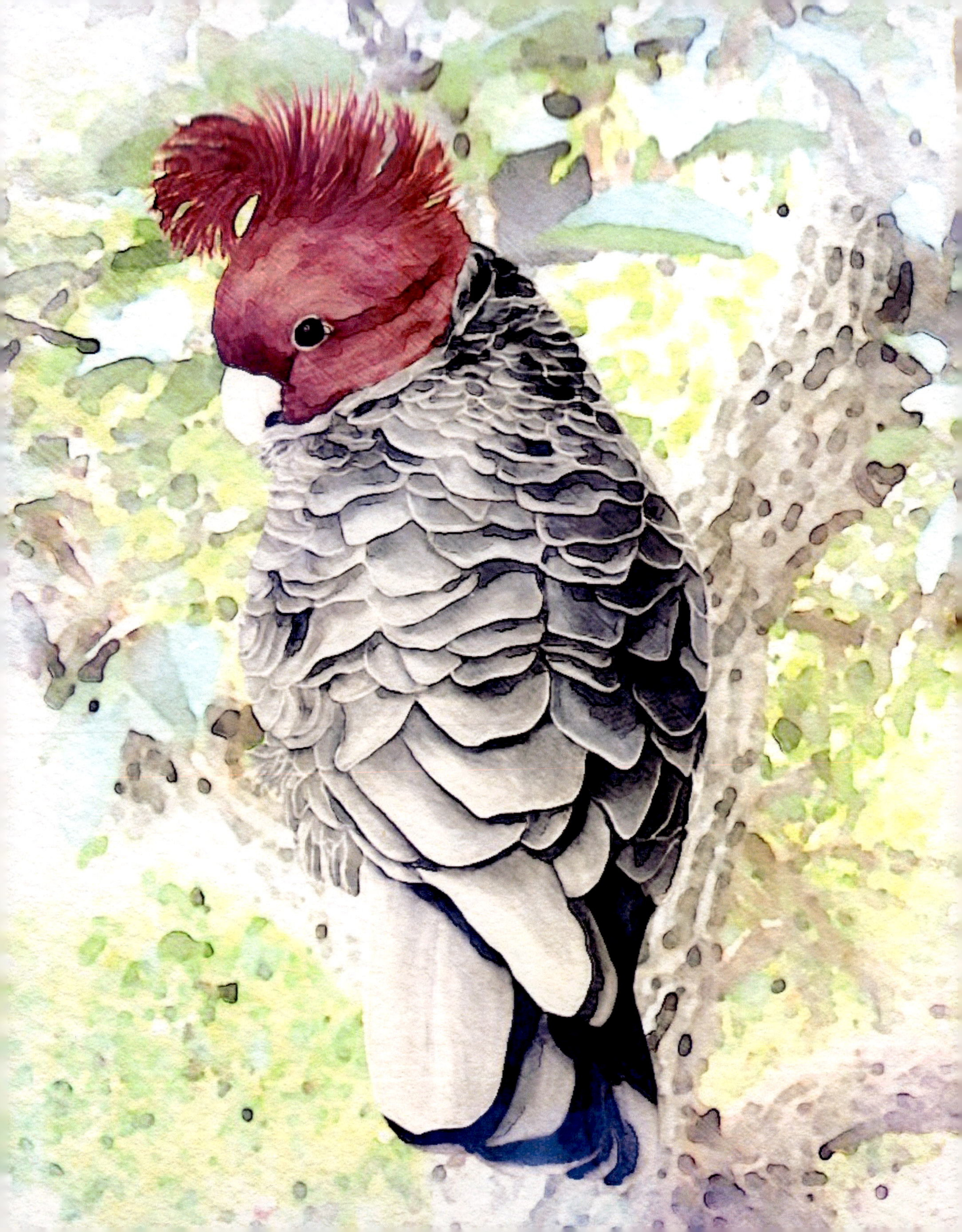

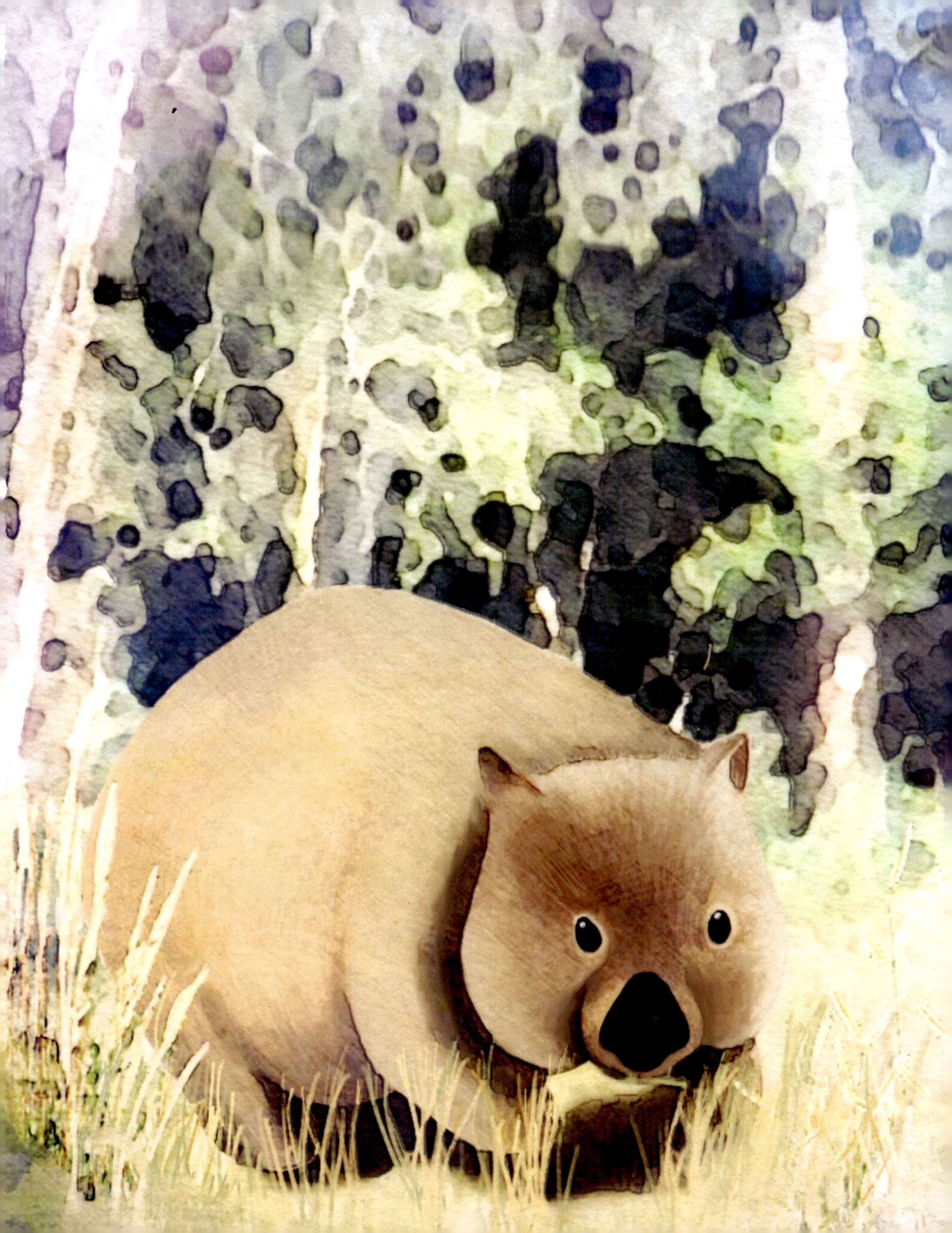

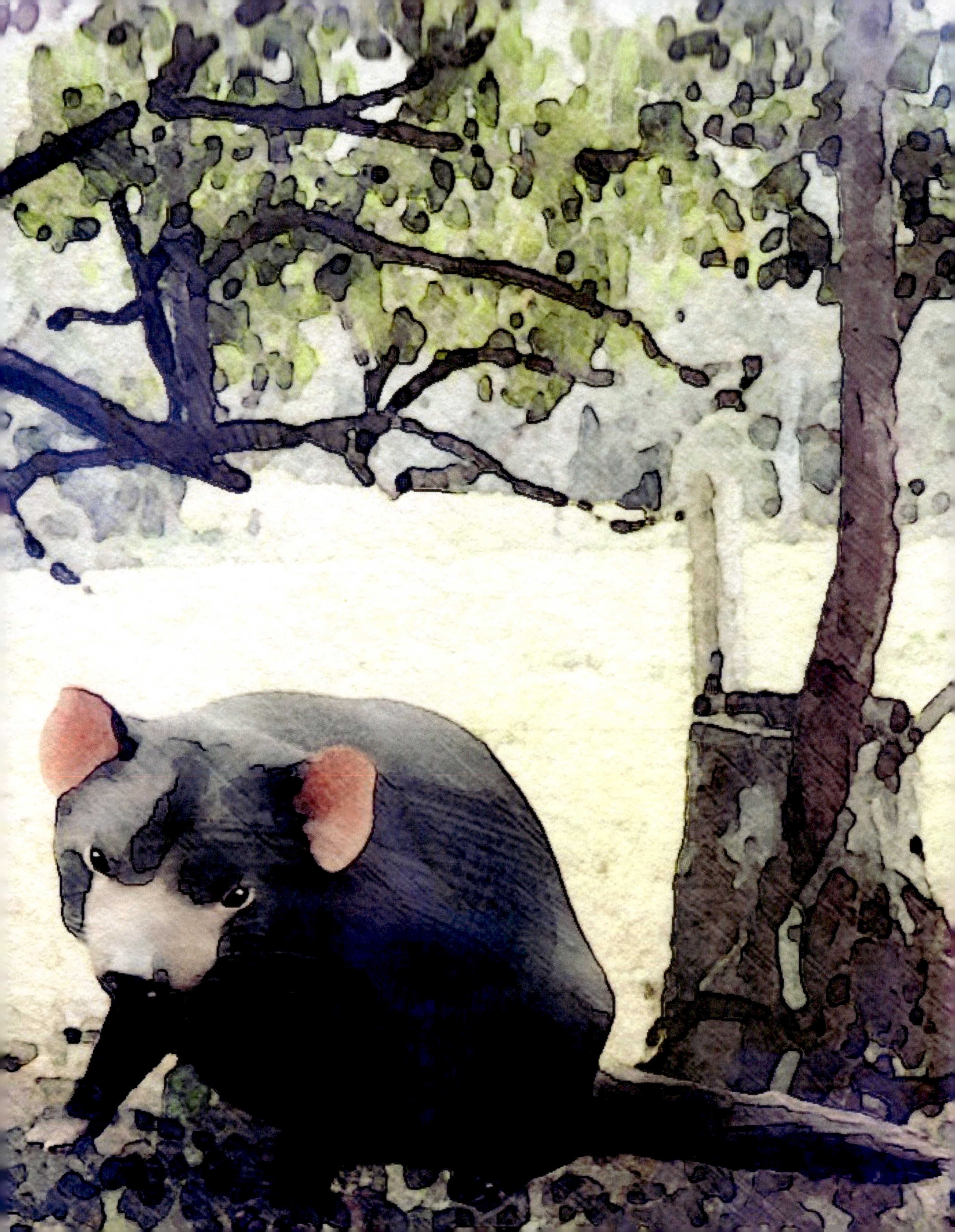

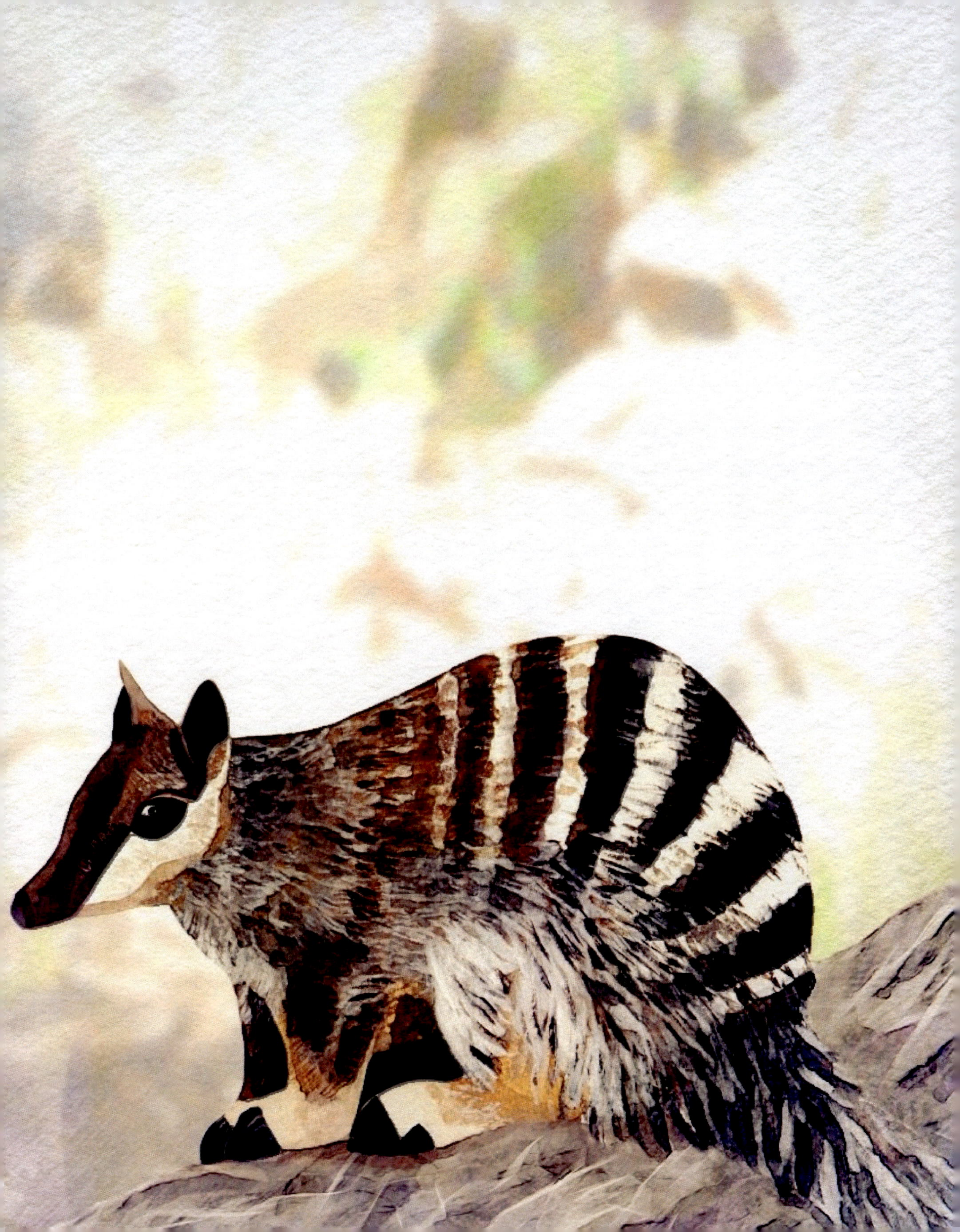

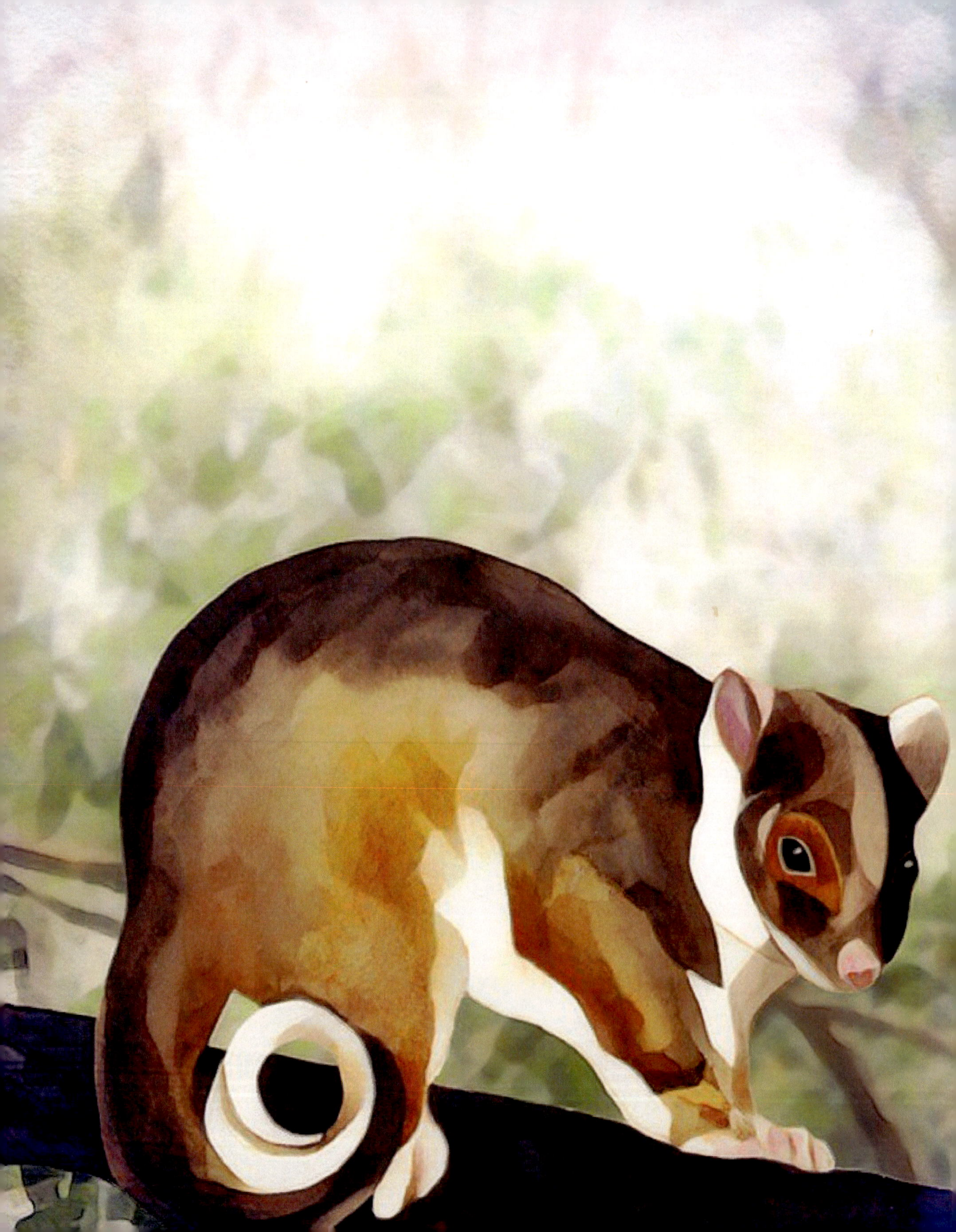

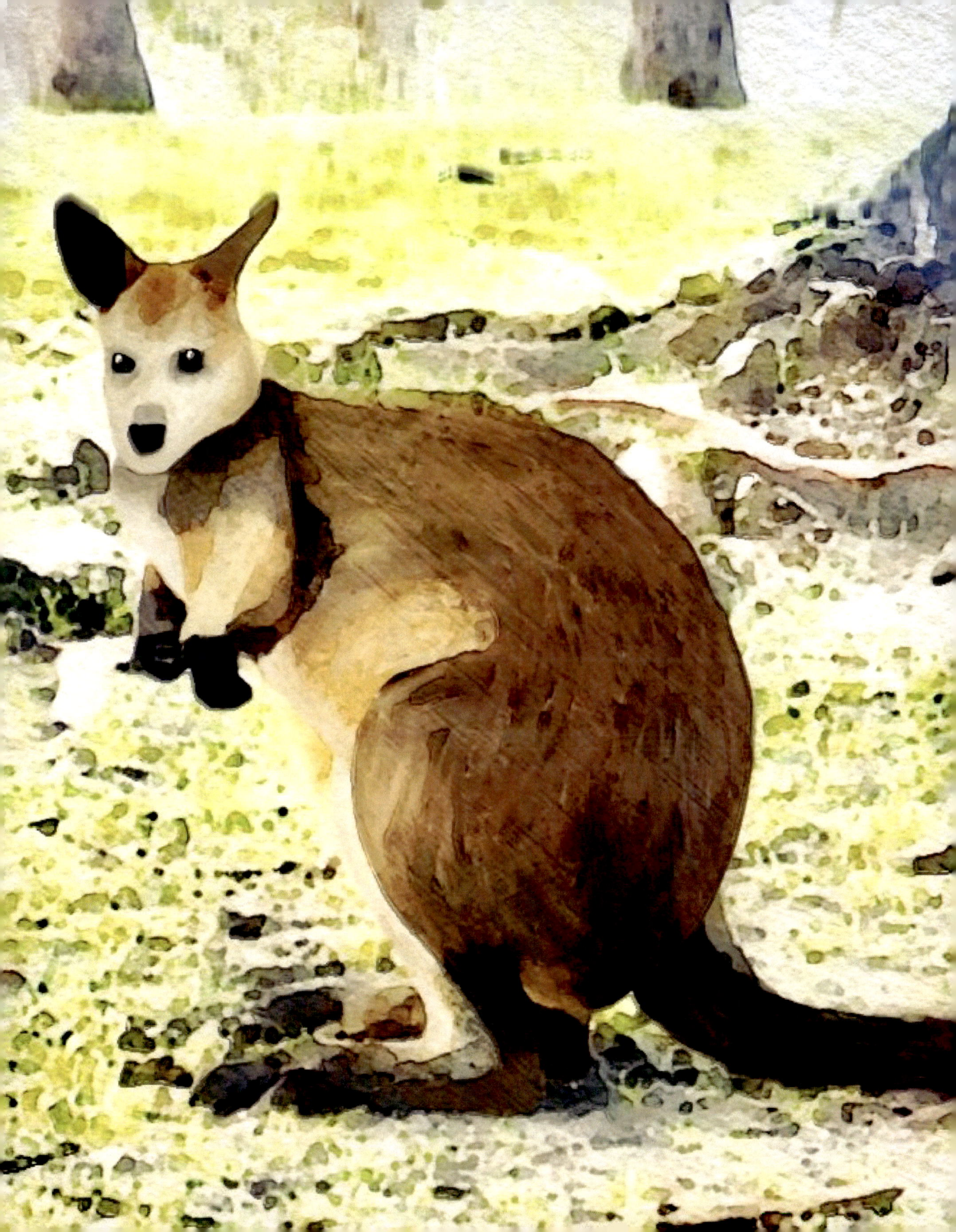

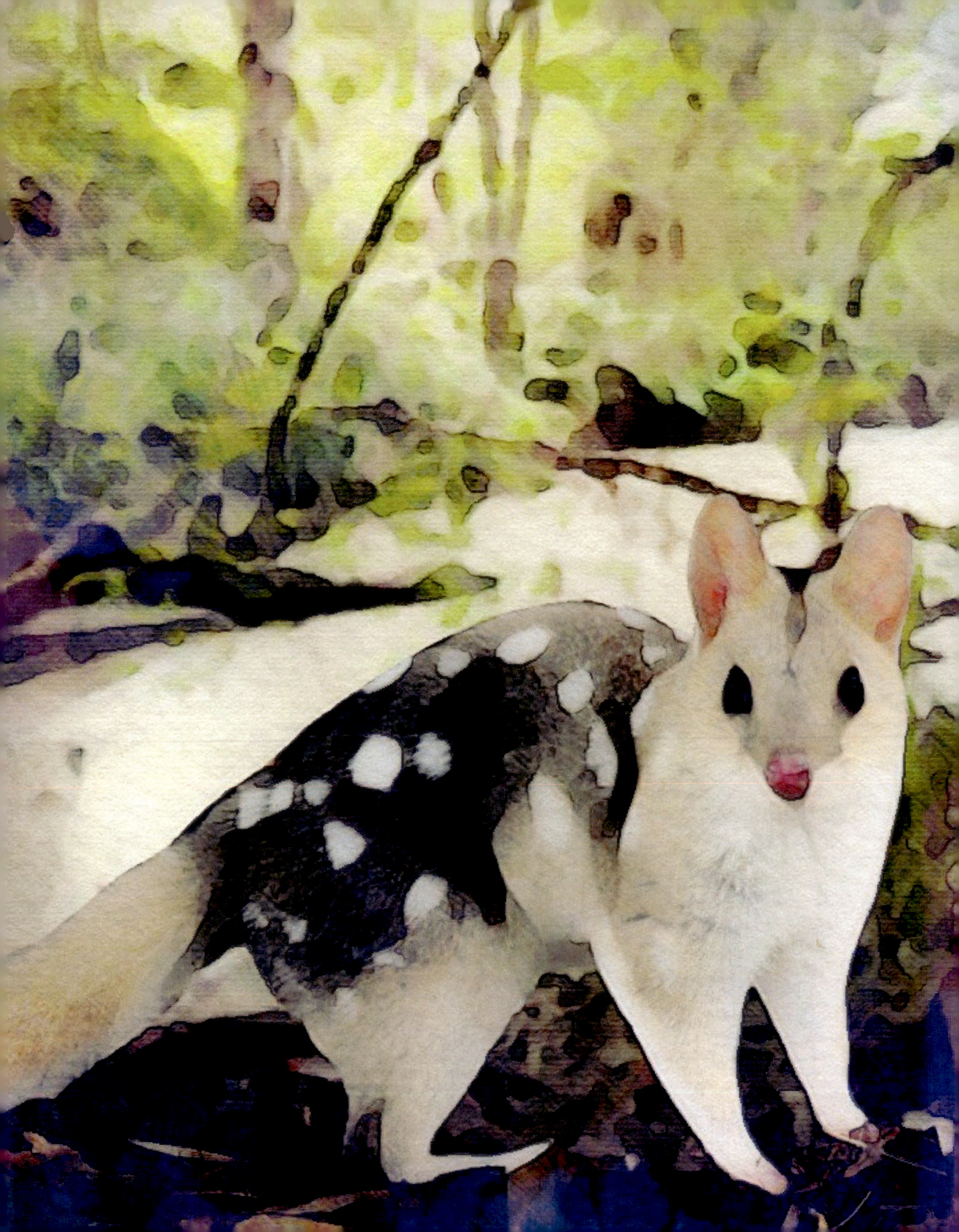

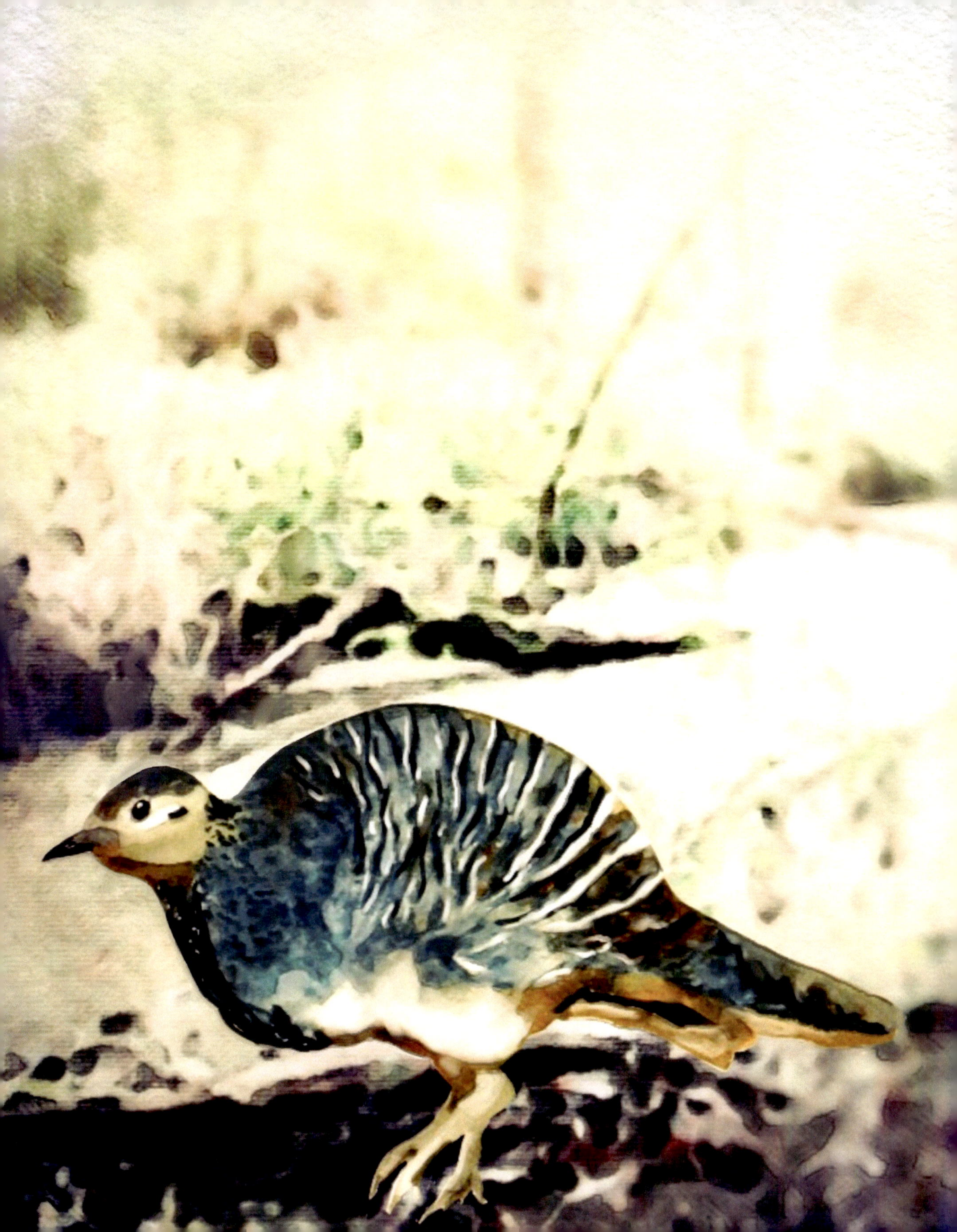

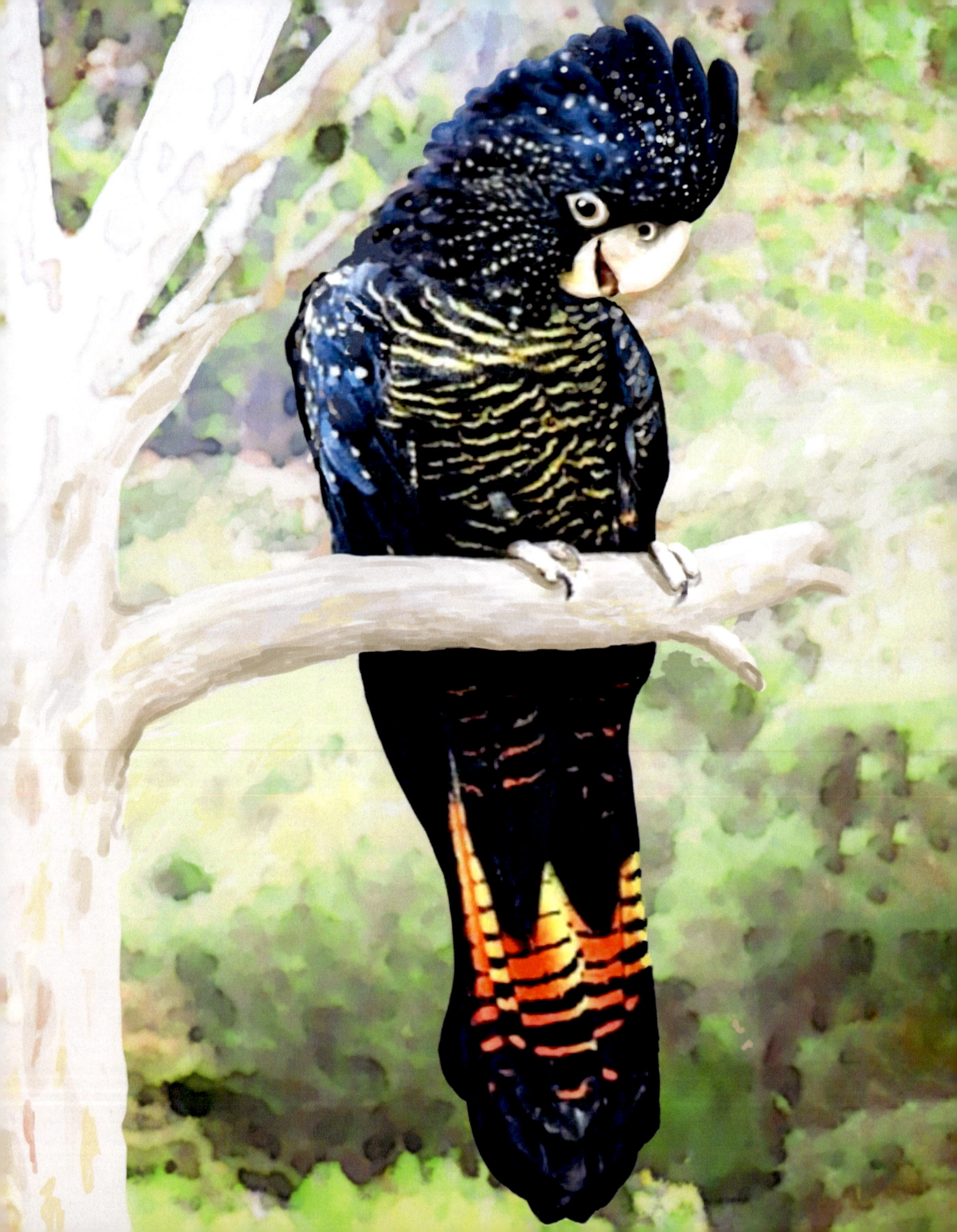

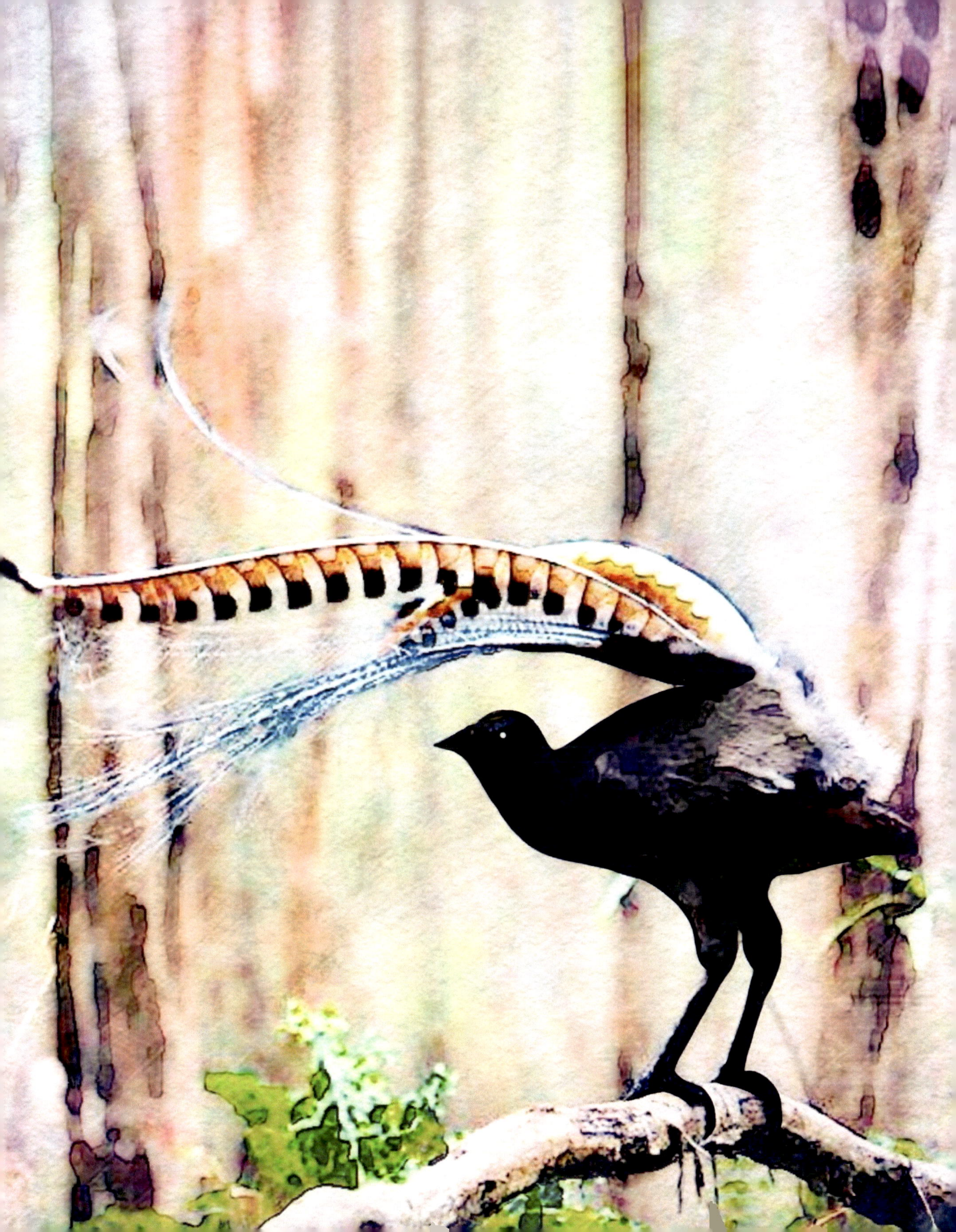

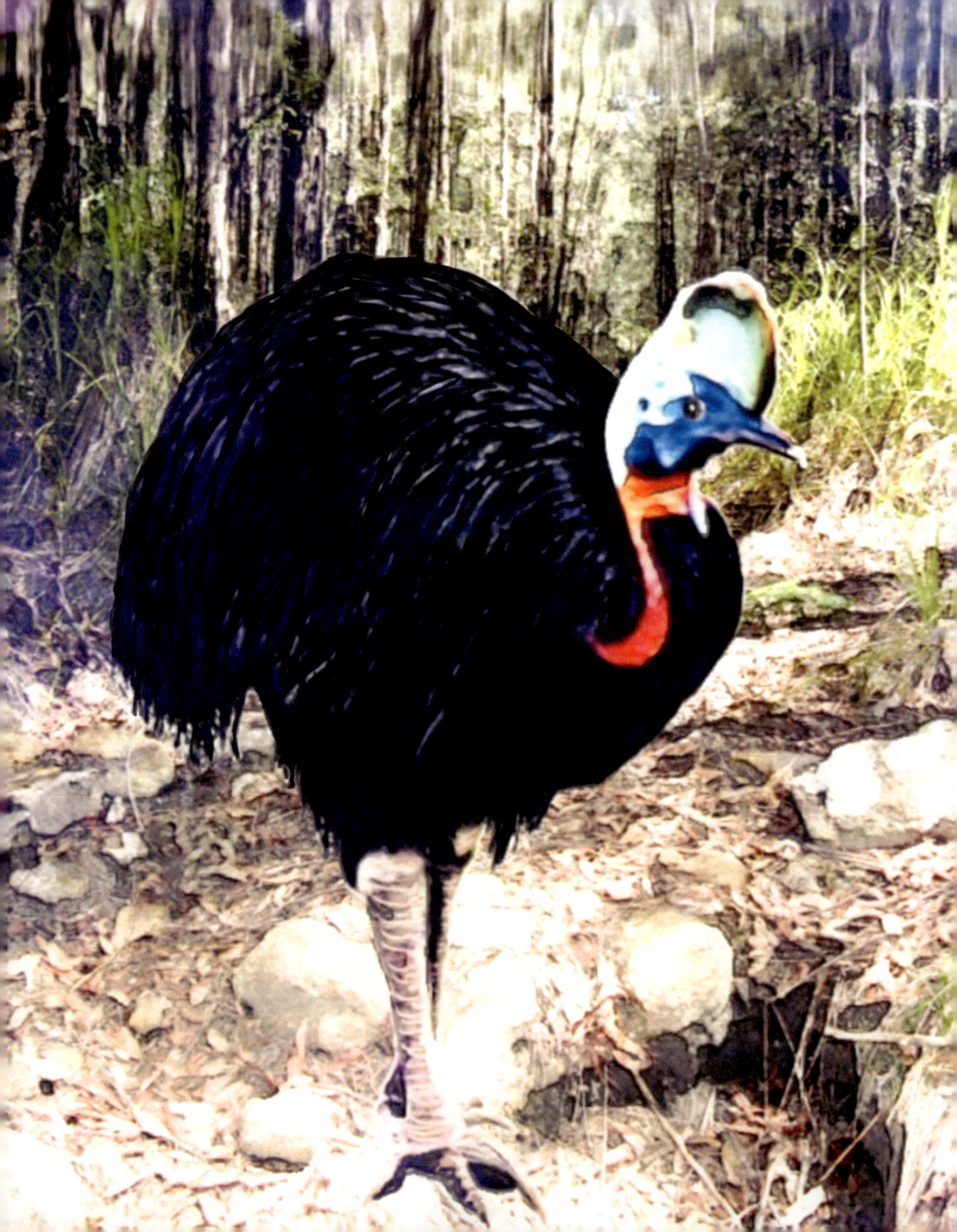

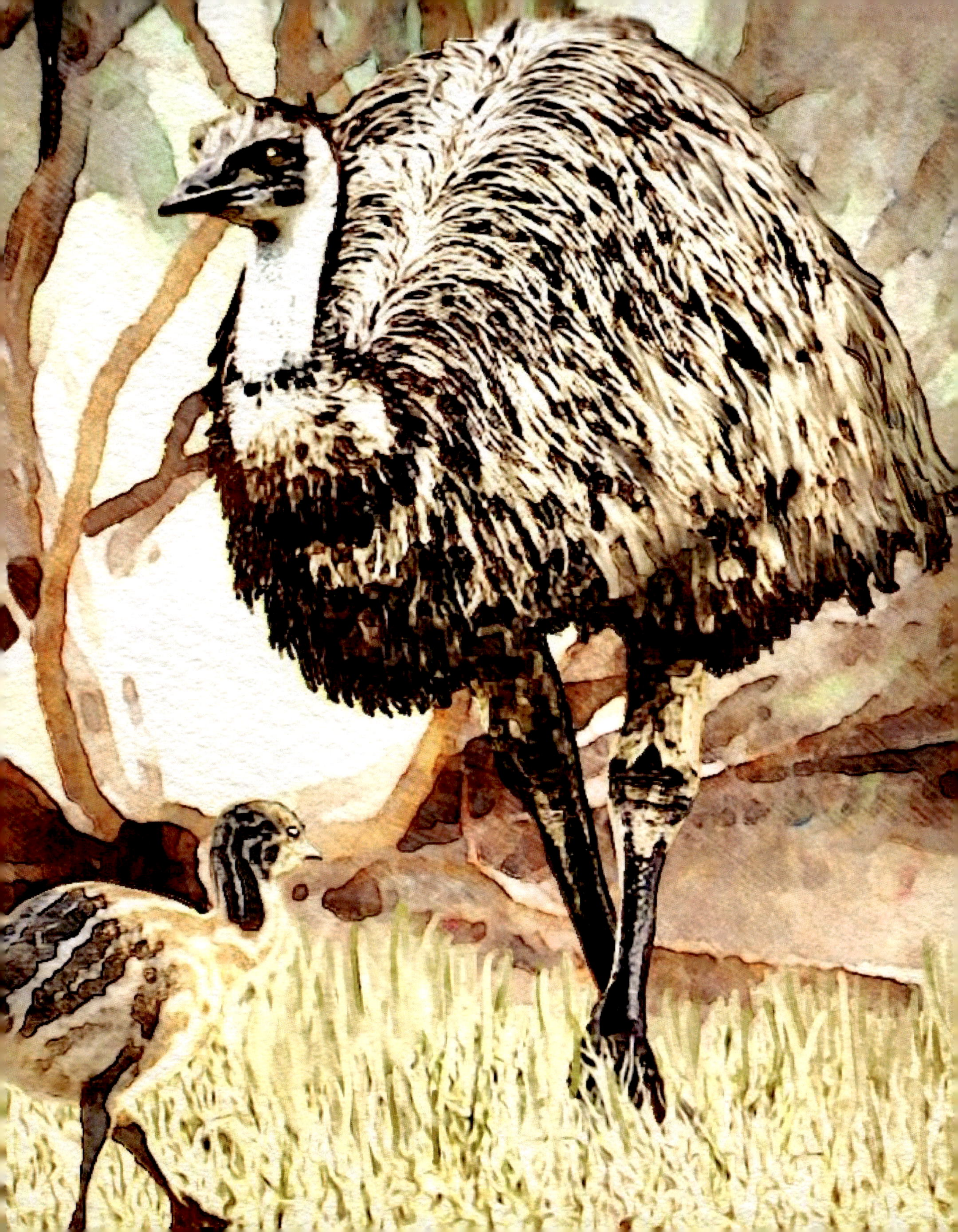

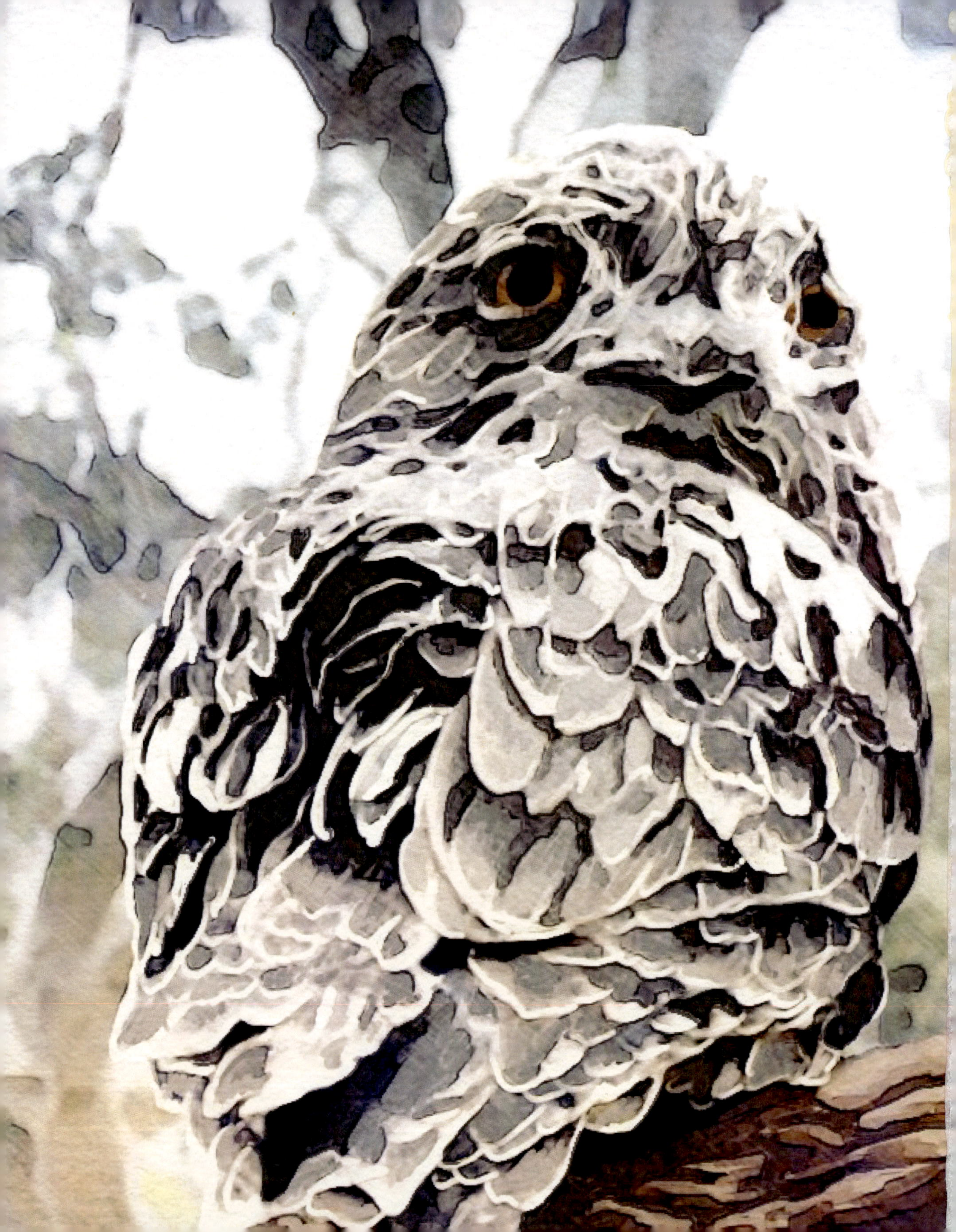

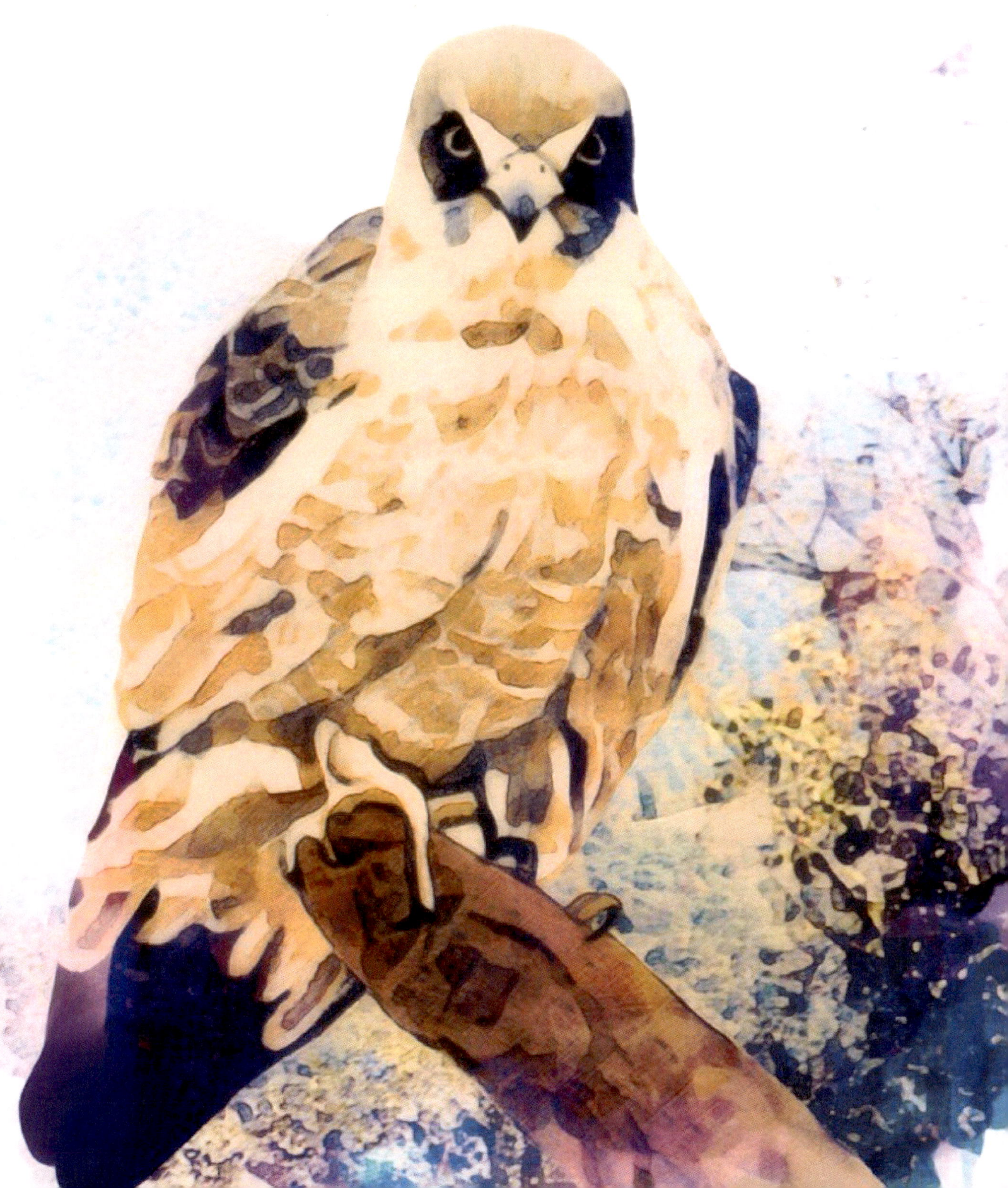

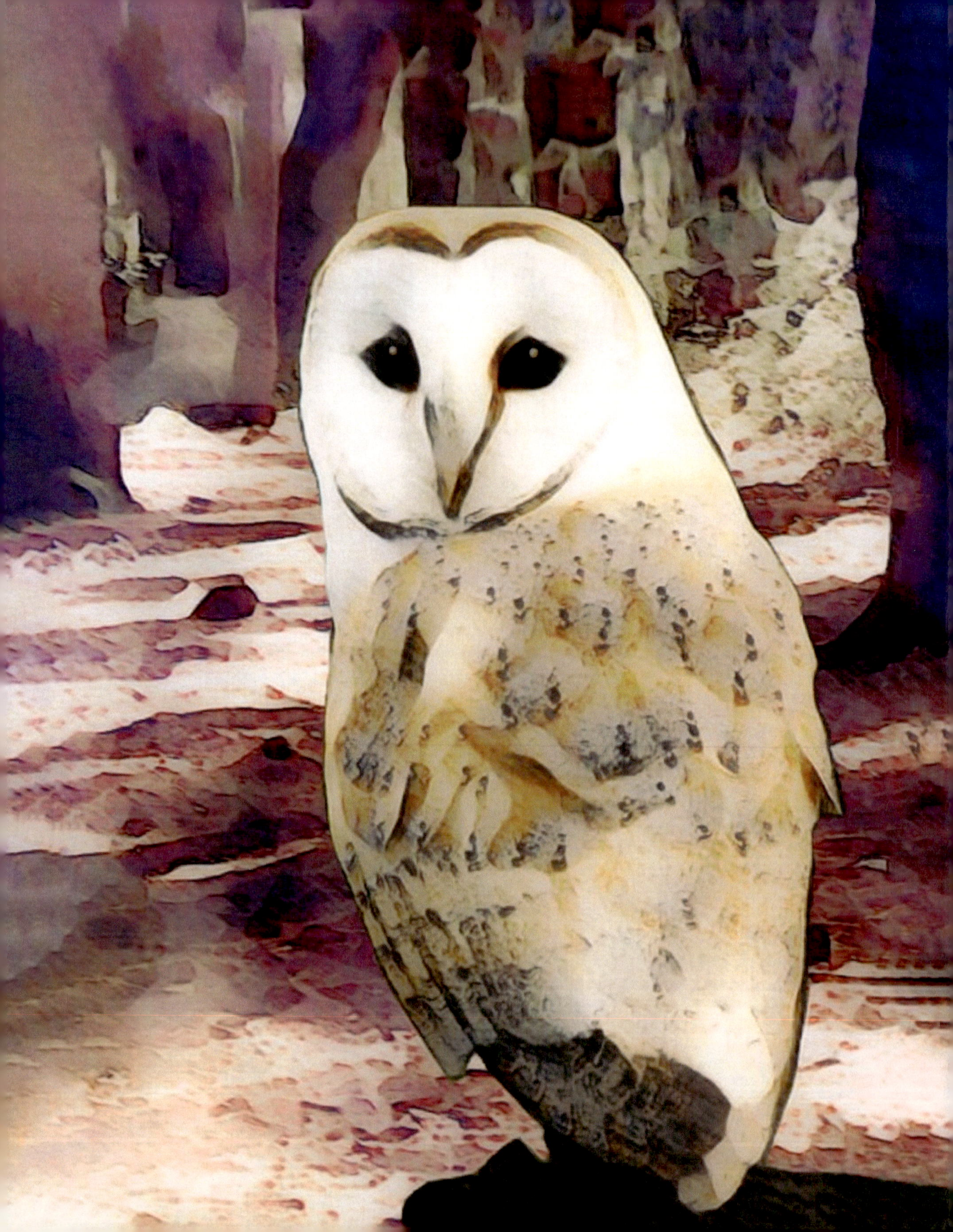

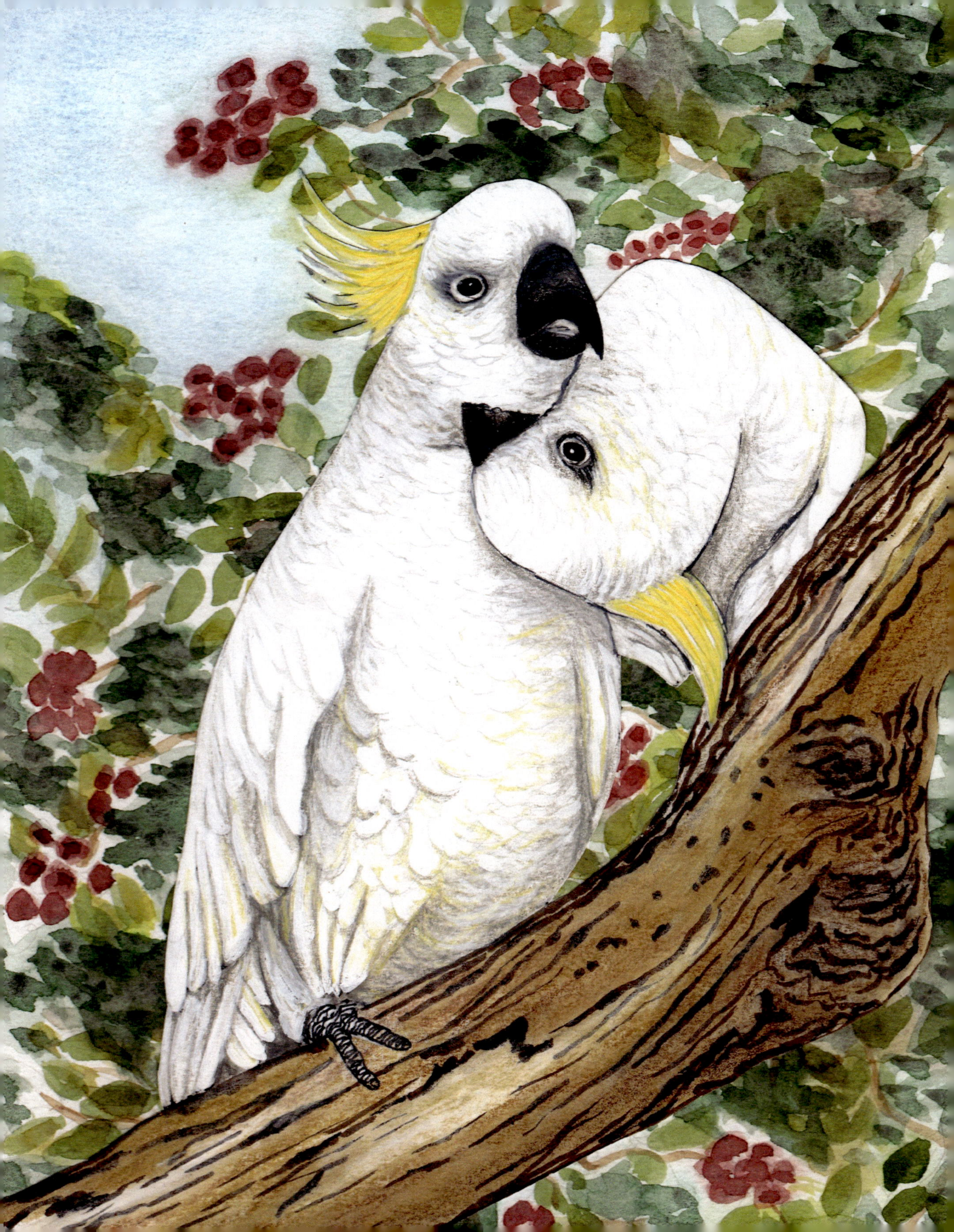

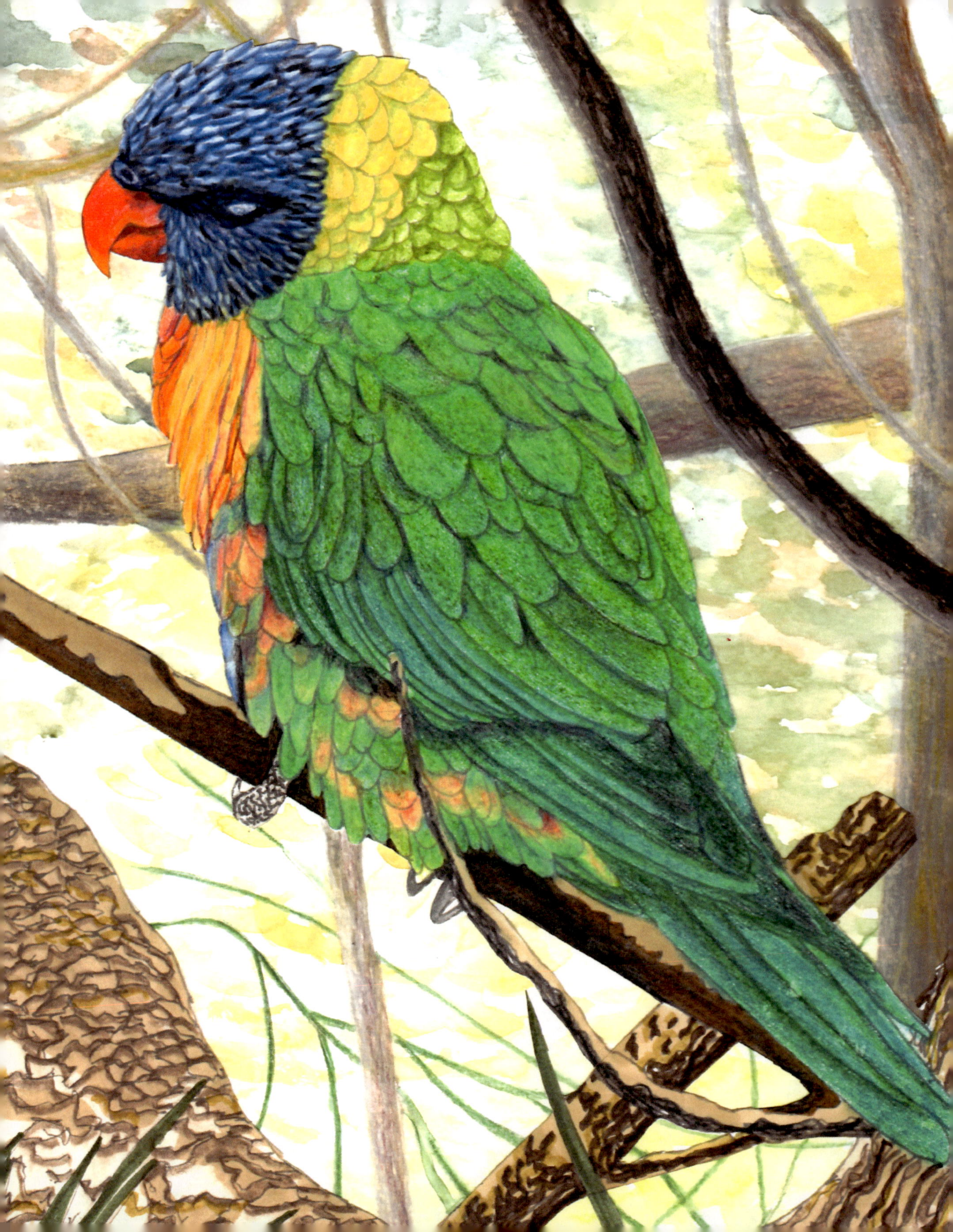

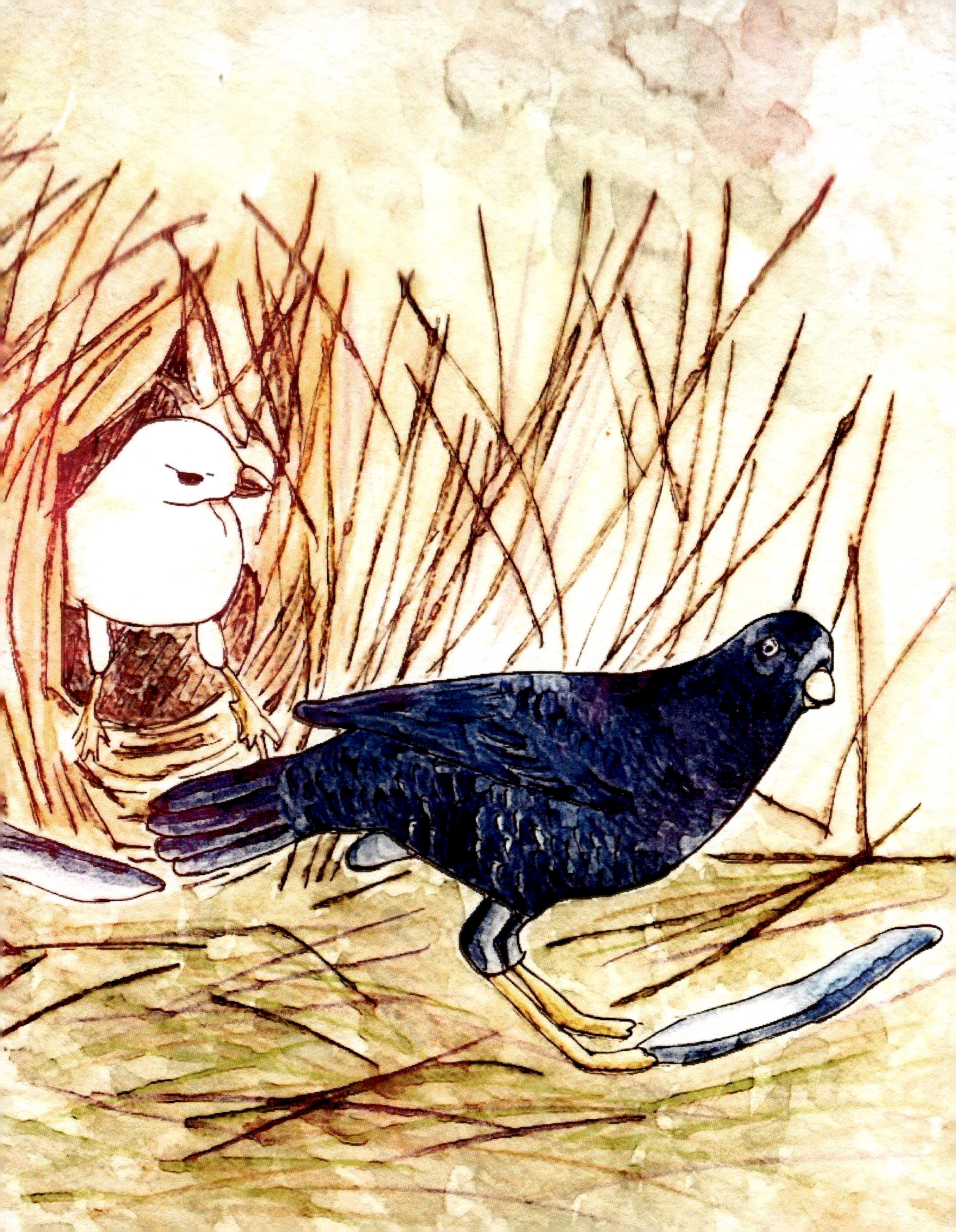

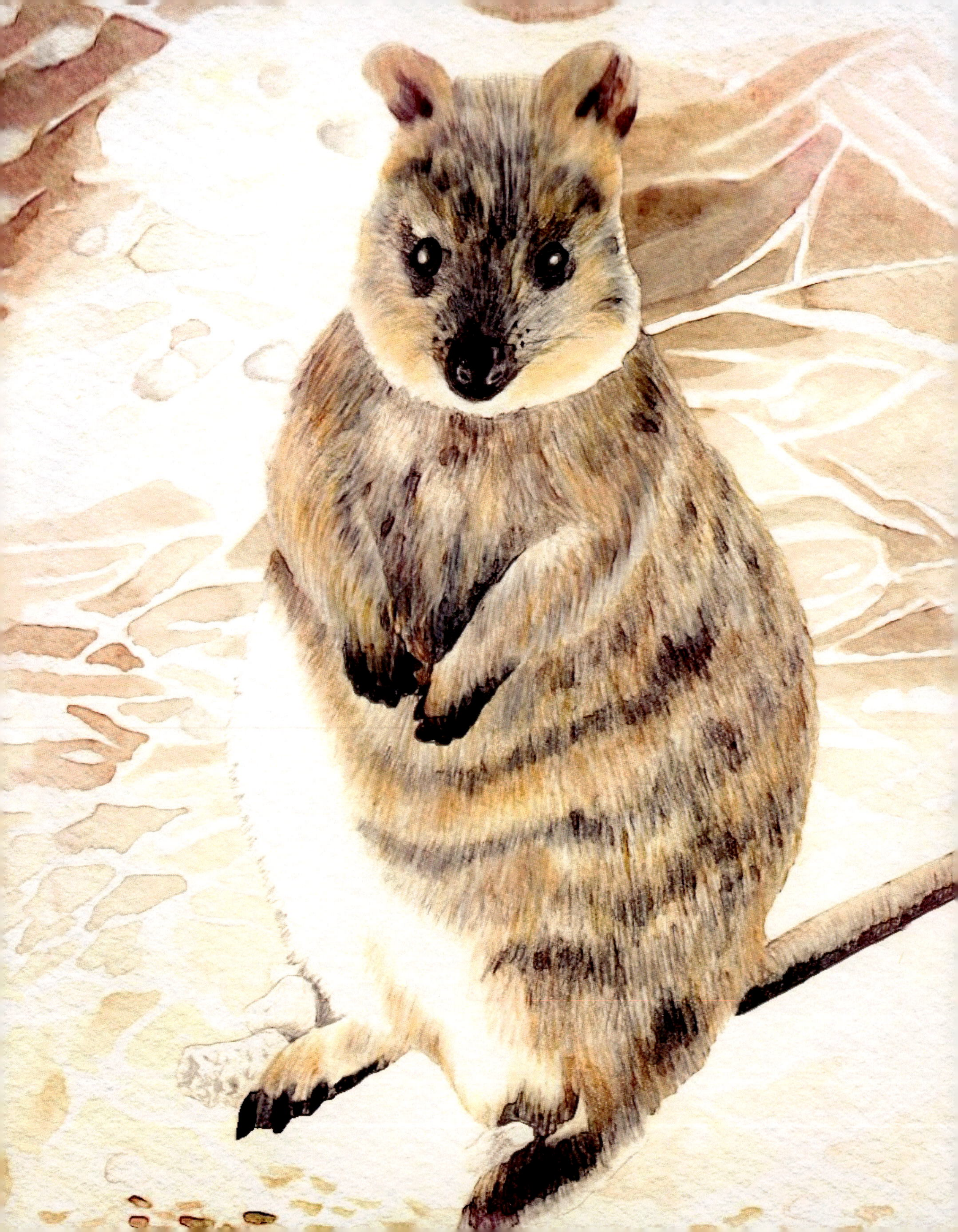

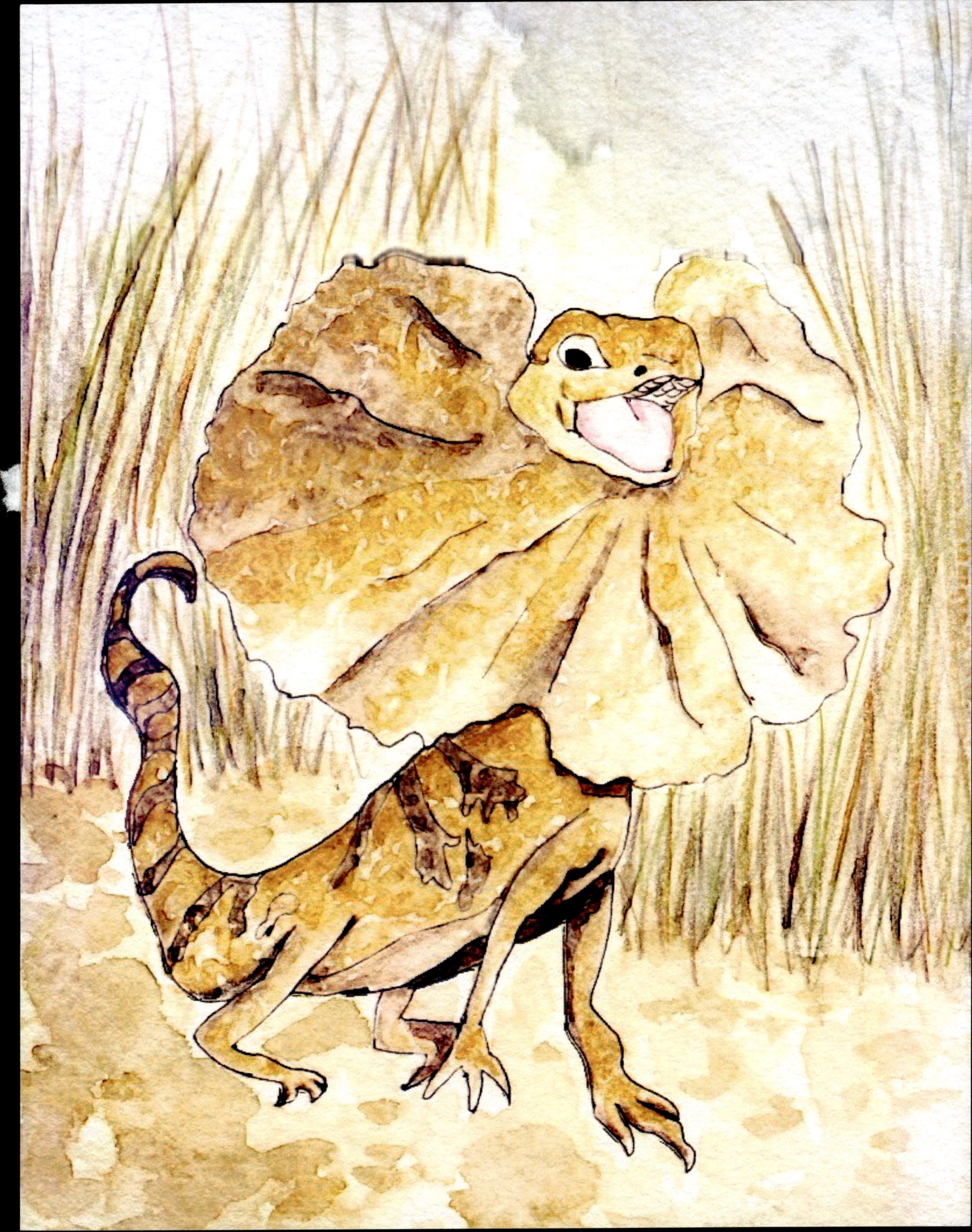

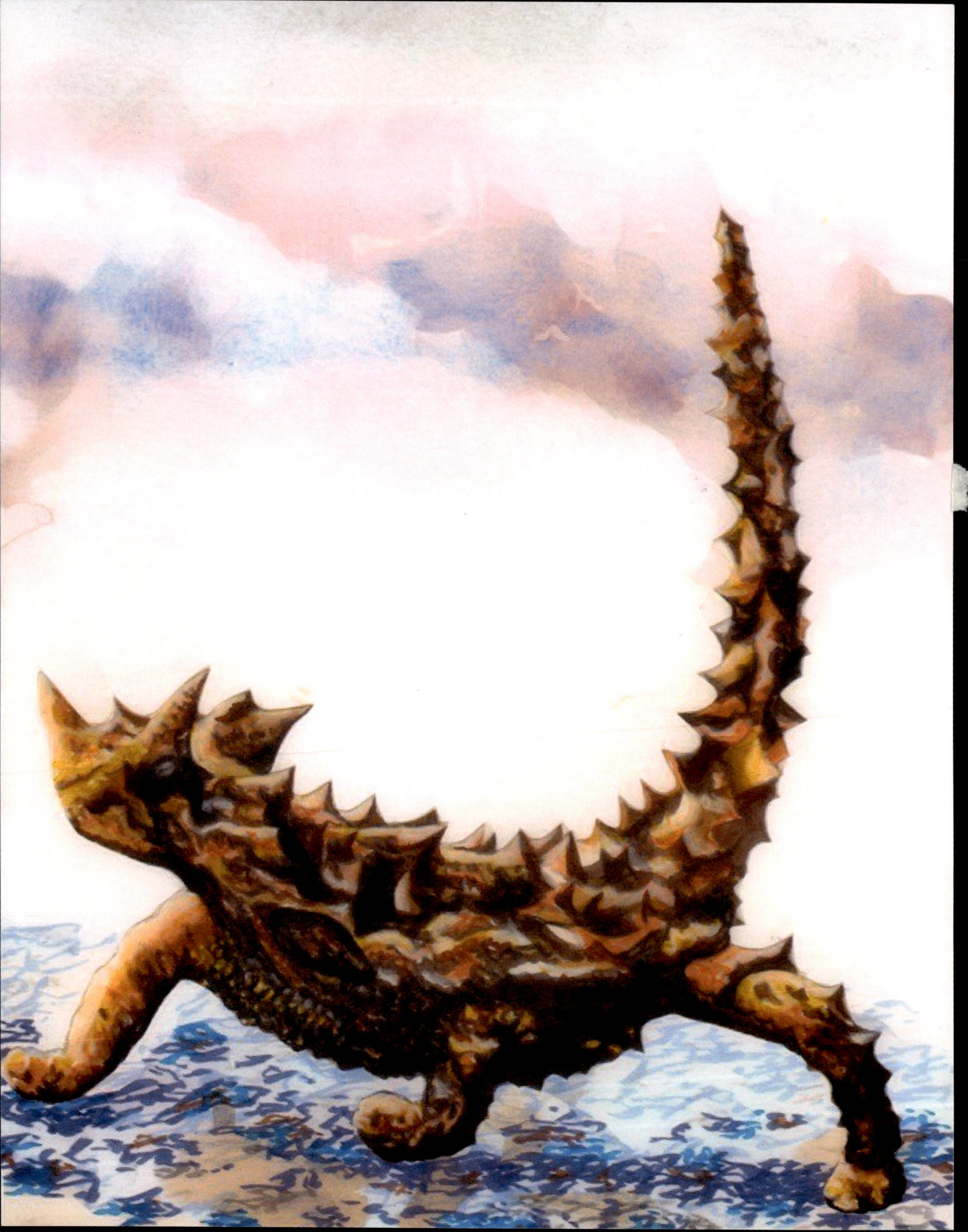

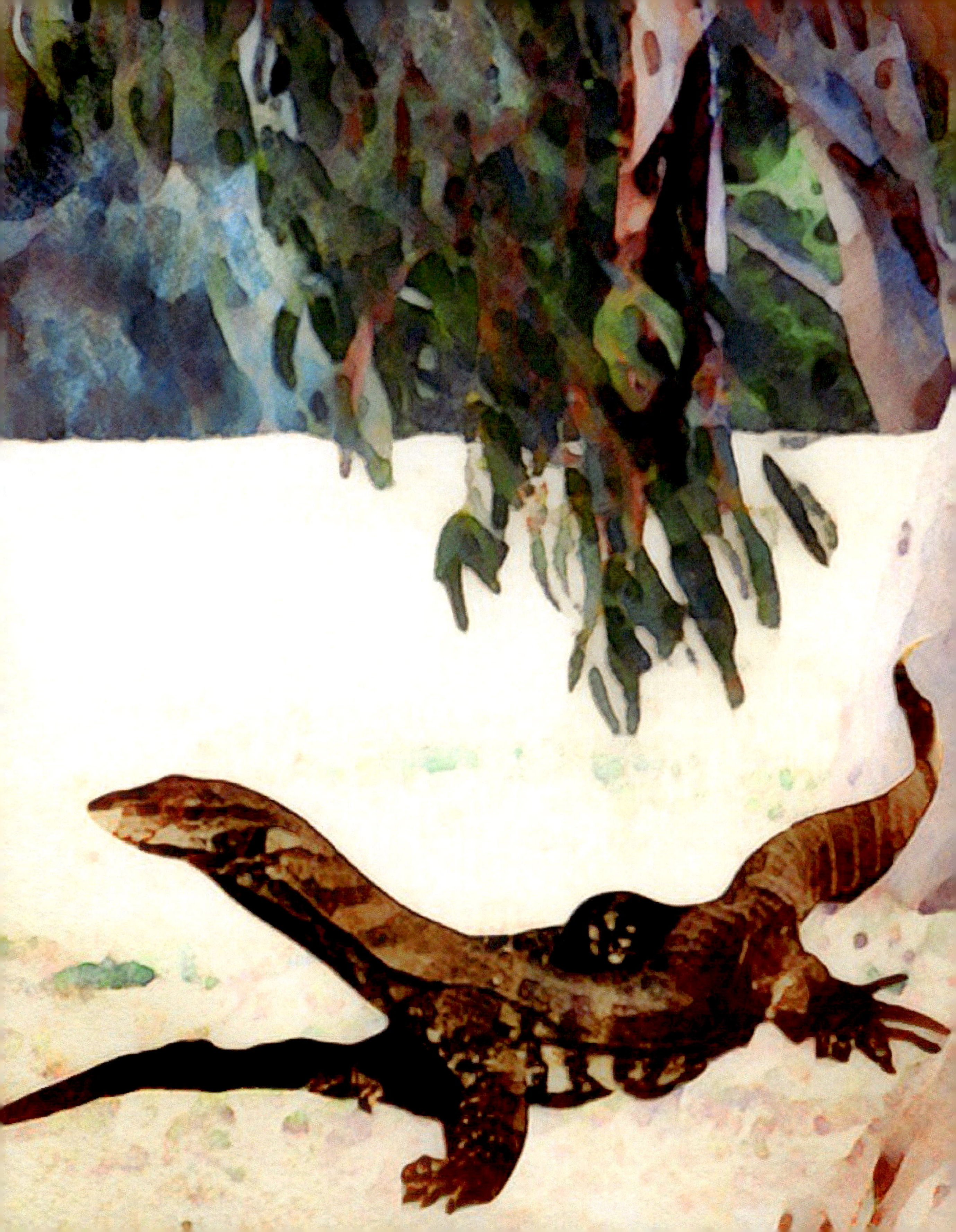

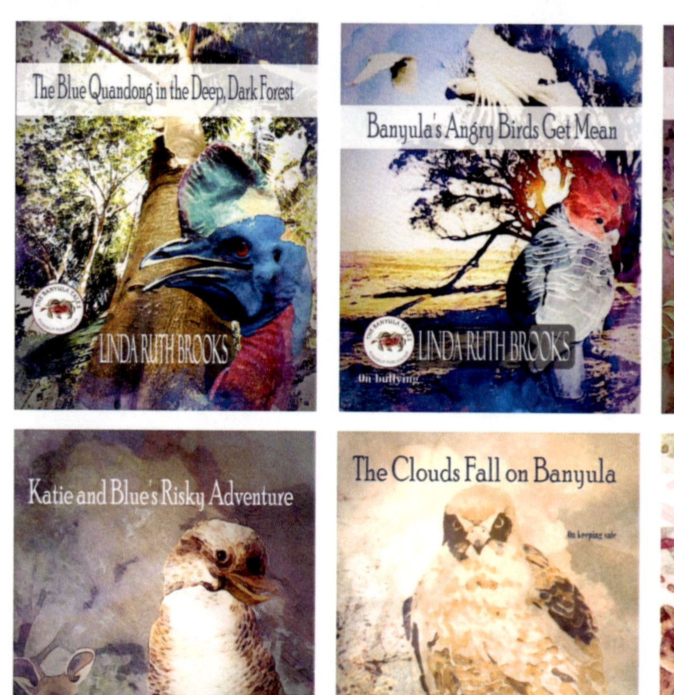

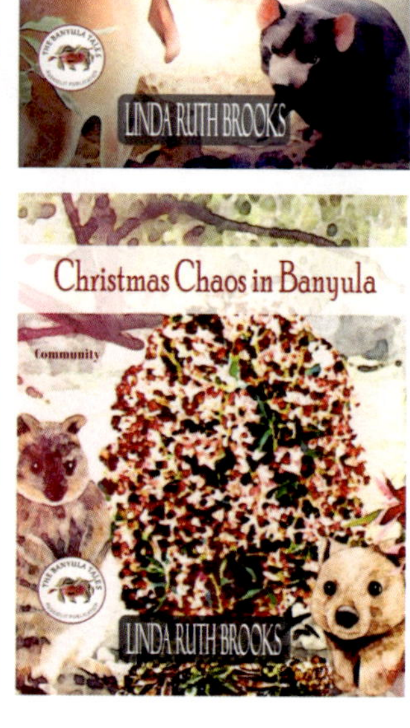

*****

Copyright © Linda Ruth Brooks 2020

All rights reserved. Without limiting the rights under copyright reserved above, no part of this work/ publication may be reproduced, stored in or introduced into a retrieval system, or transmitted, in any form or by any means (electronic, mechanical, print, photocopying, recording or otherwise), without the prior written permission of the copyright owner.

Cover Design by Linda Brooks

Original Artwork Copyright © Linda Brooks

ISBN--978-0-6484732-5-1 (Hardback)

ISBN--ISBN--978-0-6484732-6-8 (Paperback)

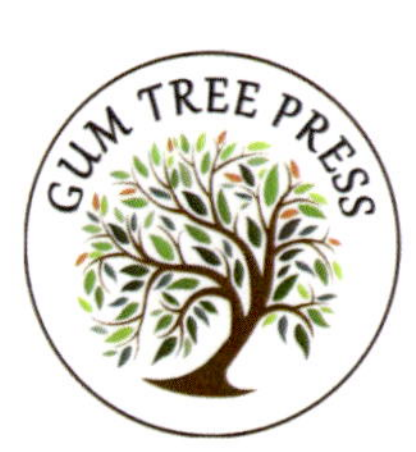

A copy of this book can be found in the National Library of Australia.

Linda's books are available through online retailers and bookstores.

Linda Brooks lives in Adelaide. She gained the attention of a publisher when her short stories found critical acclaim on the ABC website, 'The Making of Modern Australia'. Her first published book resulted, *A Curious & Inelegant Childhood,* a memoir of growing up in rural Australia. Brooks explores the gamut of human experience with fearless clarity and buoyant optimism. Her trademark wit and sharp observation is crafted with depth and compassion. Linda has written and illustrated children's' books, fiction and poetry. Linda's short stories have been published in numerous anthologies: Coastlines 5,6 &7 (Southern Cross University), Wood, Bricks & Stone (Catchfire Press) and Grieve (Hunter Writer's Centre) and Longing for Solitude (Stringybark Press). She has won creative writing awards, including first prize for The Legacy University Level Creative Writing Award and first prize for the Gabe Reynaud Creative Writing Award, and the Mater Misericordiae Grieve Writing Award. Linda's books feature her skill as an artist and illustrator.